Winter Rites

Karol Kolbusz

Cover art: *Morning Fog in the Mountains* by Caspar David Friedrich

TABLE OF CONTENTS

ACKNOWLEDGMENTS

The author would like to express his heartfelt gratitude to Ryan Dziadowiec for proofreading the entire text and suggesting additions and modifications.

INTRODUCTION

It is beyond a shadow of a doubt that the modern world is a place full of misery, suffering, and hopelessness. We are living in an atomised, rootless, and directionless society, in which nothing is valued more than frenetic money-making and shallow, carnal pleasures. Millions of people are suffering from depression, anxiety, and countless deep-seated psychological traumas.

What is the primary reason for the growing epidemic of meaninglessness and nihilism, then? It is modern man's disconnection from his own spiritual and cultural roots. The traditional teachings of ancient Greek, Roman, and Vedic philosophers and sages no longer capture his dispersed attention. The citizen of the digital century is deeply averse to spiritual authority. He is lost and sinking in the quicksands of modernity and unrestricted technological progress, which is inversely proportional to his happiness. Yet, in his arrogance, he refuses to listen to those who could potentially show him the right way. Similarly, the myths and folk tales of ancient Celtic and Germanic origin, immensely rich in meaning, depth, and beauty, are being shunned in favour of the newest blockbusters and electronic gadgets. The modern man has not just forgotten his roots, but he has also strayed away from the path of *dharma*.

Dharma can be understood as a cosmic law, with neither beginning nor end, which permeates and applies to all animate beings and inanimate objects in the universe. It is a supra-individual, metaphysical order that sets the physical world in a state of balance and harmony, protecting it from forces of chaos and dissolution. The concept of *dharma* stands in direct opposition to the current materialistic paradigm in science, according to which the universe is a mechanism devoid of any inherent meaning and purpose. The consequence of the latter worldview is ethical relativism and rejection of the notion that metaphysical principles and laws form the basis of reality. From such a limited point of view, we are born as mere pieces of flesh and bones that are left clueless and helpless in the face of the vast universe. *Dharma*, on the other hand, is a holistic natural law based on the premise that the universe is an extremely intelligent design rooted in transcendence. Many of the ancient civilisations, and particularly those of Indo-European origin, were *dharmic* in nature – meaning that all aspects of social life (religion, politics, science, law, literature, war, agriculture, etc.) within them were constructed in consonance with *dharma*. Due to obvious racial, cultural, and linguistic differences, this universal law manifested itself in a slightly divergent way in each civilisation. There was a time on Earth, however, when people across Europe and Asia were ruled by virtuous kings whose reign was strengthened by this primordial, sacred law.

In order to empower people with meaning, hope, and strength, and to contribute to the restoration of forgotten *dharmic* principles, I have decided to write the present book of haiku poetry inspired by Indo-European cultural and spiritual heritage.

Haiku is a traditional Japanese three-line poem form with seventeen syllables, written in a 5/7/5 syllable count. Often focusing on natural images, haiku stresses clarity, intensity, and directness of expression.

The purpose of this work is threefold:

1) To put the readers in a contemplative mood, which will hopefully encourage them to appreciate the beauty of nature, do more to protect the environment (lest we are deprived of its sanative power), and to slow down, despite the omnipresent obsession with speed and action. As the title of the present volume, *Wintertide Rites*, suggests, the poems are related to the themes of coldness, hibernation, slowness, introspection, death, and decay. Haiku poems, with their meaningful simplicity, are an excellent tool that can potentially help us lead a more meditative and satisfactory life.

2) To acquaint the readers with the pre-Abrahamic cultural heritage of Europe and Asia. I have chosen to take a closer look at the beliefs of the ancient Celts, Germanic peoples, Romans, and Greeks. Furthermore, the Vedic civilisation of ancient India, as well as Jain, Buddhist, Bön, and Shintō traditions have been covered in a separate section. Each haiku (with the exception of miscellaneous poems) is followed by a commentary section, which aims to explicate the meaning and significance of a given tradition, custom, historical event or a deity. The additional explanations are meant to encourage and inspire the reader to research these topics in greater depth and detail. At the end of the book, I include a list of suggested further reading.

3) To stress the crucial importance of spiritual practice and devotion to the deities in the ancient world, as well as to show how, according to the ancients, the metaphysical affected the physical. The textual and archaeological evidence from Classical Antiquity demonstrates that gods were far from being distant and indifferent, and they actively participated in the world. They were not just archetypes, symbols, and role models, but also real metaphysical beings, aspects and manifestations of the pure and

formless God. Haiku poems, with their focus on describing beautiful, yet meaningful, transitory moments can perfectly illustrate how the eternal influences the temporal.

In my opinion, the ultimate solution to the crisis of modernity is the restoration of *dharma* on all levels – which includes, quite literally, bringing the gods of our ancestors back. Naturally, this process should not be done mechanically and thoughtlessly. We must consider the reality of the modern world. That being the case, the nature of pre-Abrahamic, *dharmic* deities is perennial – they have always existed and will continue to exist, so long as the world turns. They wait to be re-discovered, for metaphysical reality is neither contingent nor subject to change.

The present work is the first volume of a seasonal tetralogy. It is my hope that those who seek beauty, knowledge, and inspiration will find *Wintertide Rites* and its sequels interesting and thought-provoking.

PART ONE

CELTIC HERITAGE

Cernunnos

The bright crescent moon
in the lush, foggy valley;
an echoing roar

Commentary

In the religion of the ancient Celts, Cernunnos is the conventional name given to a torc-wearing, horned deity, often portrayed with stag's antlers and different animals surrounding him. His name is known from the so-called Pillar of the Boatmen erected in Lutetia (modern Paris), where he is depicted among other Gallo-Roman deities. However, the best-known representation of this god appears on the Gundestrup Cauldron (1st century BCE), on which Cernunnos is sitting cross-legged. This image is comparable to the Pashupati Seal of the Indus Valley Civilization, showing another horned figure with his legs locked in the *padmasana* (lotus flower) position. It has been identified with the Vedic god Shiva, who was known as "the lord of the animals" and the patron of Yoga and meditation. Given the evidence, Cernunnos could be the divine personification of consciousness, as well as the god of fertility, nature, vegetation, and animals.

The setting of the poem is a deep, alpine valley somewhere in the very heart of ancient Celtic Hallstatt culture, in present-day Austria or Switzerland. One of the iconographical attributes of Shiva is the crescent moon, which symbolises the god's connection to the mind, as well as his association with night and mystery. On the Gundestrup Cauldron, both the horned figure and the stag have seven points on each antler, totalling in twenty-eight, a number that has clear lunar symbolism.

Temple to Arduinna

The profound silence
lingers by the boar statues
deep in the dark woods

Commentary

In ancient Gallo-Roman religion, Arduinna was the tutelary goddess of the Ardennes Forest (*Arduenna silva*, "wooded heights"), located mainly in present-day Belgium, Luxembourg, and France. She was often compared with Diana, the Roman goddess of the hunt and the moon. Arduinna was portrayed as a huntress riding a boar, with a quiver on her back and a knife in her hand. The haiku poem above depicts an imaginary, Gallo-Roman sanctuary dedicated to Arduinna. In ancient Gaul, boars were widely revered animals. The setting of the poem was inspired by Lucan's *Pharsalia*, in which the Roman poet describes a sacred grove (*nemeton*) located near Massalia:

"No bird nested in the nemeton, nor did any animal lurk nearby; the leaves constantly shivered though no breeze stirred. Altars stood in its midst, and the images of the gods... The people feared to approach the grove, and even the priest would not walk there at midday or midnight lest he should then meet its divine guardian."

Dea Artio

A thunderous roar
down in the secluded cave;
the dripstones shatter

Commentary

In ancient Gallo-Roman religion, Artio was a goddess associated with bears. Her name is derived from the Gaulish word *artos*, meaning "bear" (a possible source of the name Arthur). She was worshipped in southwestern Germany and Switzerland, especially near the Swiss city of Bern, where a votive statuette representing Artio was discovered in 1832.

The haiku poem above depicts the premature awakening of a she-bear. Something or someone, perhaps a human intruder to the cave, has disturbed her deep winter sleep, which is formally known as torpor. Contrary to popular belief, bears do not hibernate. In torpor, which is a milder form of hibernation, bears reduce their circulation, breathing, and heartbeat only to a level which allows them to defend their den at any time.

Epona

Sunset on the hills —
she watches from afar as
mares graze peacefully

Commentary

In ancient Gallo-Roman religion, Epona was a divine protectress of horses, mules, carters, and cavalry. Her name (derived from the Proto-Celtic *ekwos*, "horse") means "Great Mare". She was also a goddess of fertility and abundance (comparable to Demeter). After Gaul had been subdued by Romans the cult of Epona was spread over the western provinces of the Roman Empire. It was particularly popular among the cavalrymen (*equites*) and other people who worked with horses (e.g. farmers), as small, painted images of Epona have been found in barns and stables. According to the ancient calendar from Guidizzolo in Italy, December 18 was Epona's feast day.

Epona may have been connected to the Indo-European horse sacrifice ritual, which was associated with consecrating and strengthening a king's sovereignty. In Vedic religion, the ceremony was known under the name *Ashvamedha*. Ancient Romans observed the October Horse (*Equus October*) sacrifice ritual. Gerald of Wales, writing in the late 12th century, described the kingly inauguration ritual among the Irish, which involved symbolical coitus between the king and the mare (who may have been the sexual surrogate of the goddess of sovereignty), followed by the sacrifice of the latter.

Sanctuary of Vosegus

At the icy heights —
frozen acorns and pine cones
in the bronze vessel

Commentary

In ancient Gallo-Roman religion, Vosegus (otherwise known as Vosagus or Vosacius) was a tutelary deity of the Vosges Mountains (*Vosego silva*) in eastern Gaul. The scant evidence from inscriptions and sculptures suggests that he might have been the god of hunters and vegetation. He was worshipped in eastern Gaul and present-day western Germany. Mont Donon, the highest peak in the Northern Vosges, was the site of a sanctuary dedicated to Vosegus.

The haiku poem above depicts the said temple in winter. Acorns and pine cones are autumnal offerings to Vosegus. Since they are frozen, they also represent hibernating nature in winter. The Roman poet Lucan describes how the Gaulish druids masticated acorns in their rituals of divination. The absence of alkaloids in the acorn precludes any possible hallucinatory properties; therefore, this druidical practice may have been purely symbolical. That being the case, it is important to remember that the oak was one of the most sacred and revered trees in the Celtic tradition.

A Devotee of Gobannus

The blacksmith's silence
before the hallowed hammer
strikes the hot metal

Commentary

In ancient Gallo-Roman religion, Gobannus was a divine patron of blacksmiths and metalworking, comparable to the Roman deity Vulcan, the Welsh mythological figure Govannon, or the ancient Irish god Goibniu. One metal sheet dedicated to Gobannus was found near Bern in Switzerland. It is interesting to note that similar names were borne by some members of the Gaulish aristocracy (e.g. Vercingetorix's uncle Gobannito), indicating the tremendous importance of metalworking in ancient Celtic societies.

The haiku poem above depicts a blacksmith who honours Gobannus with a silent prayer before he proceeds with his daily routine. In this way, the final product of the blacksmith's work will be consecrated and strengthened by divine auspiciousness.

Shrine to Cissonius

Treveran merchants
offer wine at the altar;
the blizzard passes

Commentary

In ancient Gallo-Roman religion, Cissonius (also known as Cisonius or Cesonius) was a god of trade and protector of merchants, often identified with the Roman deity Mercury. His cult was popular in southwestern Germany and Belgic Gaul (inhabited by the Treverii tribe). His female counterpart or consort, the goddess Cissonia, is also recorded on inscriptions.

The haiku poem above depicts Treveran merchants, who are unable to continue their travel due to the raging blizzard. Fortunately, they happen upon a roadside shrine to Cissonius and decide to stop. They pray and offer wine to the deity, hoping that he will protect them from the undesirable weather conditions. The snowstorm becomes less severe, and eventually, it passes, allowing the pious traders to continue their travel.

Before the Battle

A cold, sleepless night —
a pious Helvetian prays
to Mars Caturix

Commentary

In ancient Gallo-Roman religion, Caturix was the war god of the Helvetii tribe (who, by the time of Roman conquest, inhabited the Swiss Plateau). His Gaulish name means "battle-king". In the *interpretatio romana*, he was identified with Mars, Roman deity of war. Several temples dedicated to Caturix have been found, including the one at Aventicum, the capital of Roman Helvetia. Another Gaulish tribe, the Caturiges, were probably named after the deity.

The haiku poem above depicts a religious Helvetian man, perhaps the leader of the aforementioned tribe, who is worried about the outcome of the upcoming battle. He offers his humble obeisances to Caturix, the war god, praying for divine assistance in the strife to come.

Abnoba's Bane

Trapped in the wire snares
a doe lays on the snowbank;
the flaming dusk falls

Abnoba's Blessing

Crepuscular gloom —
an arrow misses a fawn
fleeing down the hill

Commentary

In ancient Gallo-Roman religion, Abnoba was the tutelary goddess of the Black Forest (*Silva nigra* or *Mons Abnoba*). Iconographic sources depict Abnoba as a huntress surrounded by different animals such as a hare, a stag, and a hound, making her a Gaulish equivalent of the Roman goddess Diana. Several epigraphic inscriptions and altars related to Abnoba have been found. The haiku poems above illustrate two different aspects of the goddess. On the one hand, she has the power to control the forest population and to bestow blessings upon hunters by taking away the lives of animals. On the other hand, Abnoba has the ability to rescue forest animals from different perils, moderating our human desire to conquer nature. In summary, Abnoba may be seen as the divine protectress of sylvan balance.

Avaricum

A rooster's crowing —
fog rolls in from the marshes
and blankets the hill

Commentary

Avaricum (near the present-day city of Bourges) was the main *oppidum* (fortified settlement) of the Bituriges (meaning "kings of the world" or "kings of blacksmithing"), one of the most powerful Gaulish tribes. In 52 BCE, during Vercingetorix's uprising, the city was successfully besieged by Julius Caesar, which was followed by a massacre of the inhabitants. The hillfort was surrounded by a river and swamps.

The haiku poem above depicts an early winter morning in Avaricum. The Gallic rooster is one of the unofficial symbols of France. The idea originated from the play on words in Latin between *Gallus*, meaning "an inhabitant of Gaul", and *gallus*, meaning "rooster".

Hermetic Teachings

A secluded glade
under the star-studded sky;
dim shapes behind trees

Commentary

The traditional world clearly distinguished between exoteric and esoteric knowledge. The exoteric surface of philosophical or religious doctrines was available to all, whereas the esoteric depth was transmitted orally by a spiritual teacher to an exclusive group of initiates. Classical writers report that the Celtic doctrine of druidism was secret, taught in secluded places such as woodland glades and caves, and the novices had to memorize a great number of verses before they could be initiated. The druids were also skilled astronomers and astrologists. The haiku poem above depicts druidical disciples gathering in secrecy for an astronomy lesson.

The Battle of Octodurus

The heavy blizzard
merges with hailing *pila*;
the Gauls start their charge

Commentary

In the winter between 57-56 BCE, a battle took place at the alpine town of Octodurus (Martigny in Switzerland), which was at that time occupied by Romans. A conjoined army of the Seduni and Veragri Gaulish tribes assaulted the Roman fortifications. Though the Gaulish attack was unsuccessful, the intense battle resulted in the Roman army retreating out of the Alps.

Pilum (plural: *pila*) was a 2-metre javelin, a standard weapon in the equipment of ancient Roman soldiers. It consisted of an iron shank joined to wooden shaft. This weapon could be used for both throwing and thrusting.

Aremorica

A remote cliff-fort;
angry squalls of rain and snow
lash the lone watchman

Commentary

In ancient times, Aremorica (or Armorica, meaning "place by the sea") was the name given to the northwestern part of Gaul which included Brittany. In 56 BCE, Julius Caesar led a successful naval campaign against one of the main socio-political forces in Aremorica – the Venetii peoples, who were known for their powerful fleet, as well as remote and inaccessible cliff-top strongholds. According to Caesar's reports, the Venetii maintained regular trade and military contacts with the Celtic tribes of southern Britain, especially with the Dumnonii of Cornwall and Devon. In the sub-Roman period, a kingdom of Domnonée was founded in the province of Aremorica directly across the English Channel, indicating an ancient connection of peoples along the western Atlantic seaboard.

Albion

At the white, chalk cliffs —
an old druid's brooding gaze
falls on the rough sea

Commentary

In ancient times, *Albion* (possibly derived from Proto-Celtic *Albiū*, meaning "white") was the name given by Greek and Roman authors to the island of Britain. According to one theory, the White Cliffs of Dover, one of the most picturesque parts of the British coastline, might have inspired the name *Albion*. It is believed that the Scottish Gaelic word which is still used for Scotland today, *Alba*, is ultimately derived from the Brythonic *Albion*.

The haiku poem above depicts an old Brythonic druid (druids were traditionally portrayed as white-cloaked) who was recently informed about the failure of Vercingetorix's revolt against Roman rule in Gaul. The elder's meditative gaze reveals his concern over the future of his tribesmen. His worries were justified – the Romans eventually conquered the southern part of Britain a century later.

Temple to Sulis

A lead curse tablet
lays at the marble altar
amid vapour trails

Commentary

In ancient Romano-British tradition, Sulis was an originally Celtic goddess worshipped at the thermal springs of Bath, which the Romans called *Aquae Sulis* (meaning "the waters of Sulis"). She was later syncretised with the Roman goddess Minerva. At the temple to Sulis in Bath, archaeologists have uncovered many curse tablets offered to Sulis. These inscribed pieces of lead were used for asking a deity for favours, usually the restitution of stolen goods and punishing perpetrators of the crime. According to some scholarly interpretations, Sulis may have been a solar deity as her name's etymology (related to words for sun and eye) connects her with the healing energy of the sun.

Glastonbury Tor

An empty orchard —
the dying rays of the sun
on the queen's flushed face

Commentary

Glastonbury Tor, a prominent hill in the English county of Somerset, has been traditionally (since at least the 12th century) associated with King Arthur, his wife Queen Guinevere, and the Isle of Avalon (meaning "the isle of apple trees"). The evidence from archaeological excavations suggests that the site has been frequently visited and possibly occupied since the Neolithic times. The Celtic name of the hill was *Ynys Gutrin*, meaning "Isle of Glass". The earliest wooden church, which was dedicated to Saint Michael, is estimated to have been erected on the hill in the 11th or 12th century. Glastonbury Tor is topped by the roofless Saint Michael's Tower, the only remains of a stone church from the 14th century. Each New Year, the ancient custom of wassailing is celebrated in the orchard beneath Glastonbury Tor. The celebration includes drinking apple cider and singing to trees in the hope of a good harvest.

Cadbury Castle

The dragon standard
flutters in a gentle breeze;
stillness of the dawn

Commentary

Cadbury Castle is a hillfort in the English county of Somerset. The results of archaeological excavations, famously conducted by Professor Leslie Alcock in the 1960s, indicated human occupation of the hill from the late Neolithic times until the sub-Roman period (c. 420-600) of the late Iron Age. Some traditions associate Cadbury Castle with the semi-legendary King Arthur and his court at Camelot. *Y Ddraig Goch*, The Red Dragon, which is the national symbol of Wales, may have been the battle standard among the Romano-British kings. It has been suggested that the design was possibly derived from the *draco*, a military banner of the late Roman cavalry. The Greek military historian Arrian describes the *draco* in his work *Technē Taktike*, a treatise on Roman cavalry and martial tactics:

"The Scythian banners are *dracontes* held aloft on standard-length poles. They are made of coloured cloths stitched together, and from the head along the entire body to the tail, they look like snakes. When the horses bearing these devices are not in motion, you see only variegated streamers hanging down. During the charge is when they most resemble creatures: they are inflated by the wind, and even make a sort of hissing sound as the air is forced through them."

Stonehenge

A white-cloaked old man
amidst the hoar-frosted stones;
dense fog wraps the plain

Commentary

Contrary to popular belief, Stonehenge was built long before the Celts arrived in Britain, meaning any links between its construction and druids are fanciful. Yet, this monumental site must have attracted people's attention throughout the ages, including the Celtic period. Therefore, it would not be far-fetched to suggest that druids (who were traditionally depicted as white-cloaked religious leaders, though their societal role extended to that of historians, judges, astronomers, and teachers) may have used Stonehenge for ritual purposes.

Boadicea

Snowflakes on her neck —
the wind ruffles her red hair
in the blaze of dusk

Commentary

Boadicea (also known as Boudica or Boudicca), was a female ruler of the Celtic Icenii tribe (who inhabited the eastern part of Britain). She was the leader of an unsuccessful revolt against Roman invaders in AD 61 or 60. The Roman historian, Cassius Dio described her physical appearance as follows:

"In stature she was very tall, in appearance most terrifying, in the glance of her eye most fierce, and her voice was harsh; a great mass of the tawniest hair fell to her hips; around her neck was a large golden necklace; and she wore a tunic of diverse colours over which a thick mantle was fastened with a brooch."

Cynddylan's Hall

Growing murk conceals
dry tears on her pallid face;
snowflakes in the hearth

Commentary

One of the most evocative images of grief can be found in an early Welsh poem called *Canu Heledd*. Cynddylan was a prince from the Romano-British kingdom of Powys. He and his brothers were slain in battle against the Angles of Northumbria. The poem is a lament of Cynddylan's sister, Heledd, who mourns the death of her kinsmen and the dilapidation of her home:

Cynddylan's hall is dark tonight
without a fire, without a bed.
I will weep for a while, afterwards I will fall silent.

Cynddylan's hall is dark tonight
without a fire, without a candle.
Except for God, who will give me sanity?

Cynddylan's hall is dark tonight
without a fire, without a light.
Grief comes to me because of you.

Saint Nectan's Glen

A hermit's prayer
muffled by the waterfall;
soft snow on the moss

Commentary

Saint Nectan was a 5th-century southwestern Brythonic hermit, traditionally associated with a secluded woodland glen (near Tintagel in Cornwall), which was named after him. It is believed that he had his hermitage above the waterfall, the glen's most spectacular and picturesque feature of natural interest. Moss and ferns grow on the rocks surrounding the waterfall. According to the hagiographic sources, Nectan owned a small silver bell which he kept in a high tower. He would ring it during stormy weather in order to warn ships that would otherwise have been smashed on the rocks at the mouth of the Rocky Valley. Yearning for solitude, the early medieval Irish and Brythonic hermits often sought out remote and serene places of pristine beauty.

Olwen

Shafts of silver light
glimmer on her lacy dress
as she holds a bun

Commentary

In Welsh mythology, Olwen is the main female character of the legend *Culhwch and Olwen*. Her name, meaning "fair footprint", refers to her gentleness and fragility. According to the tale, wherever she walked white trefoil flowers sprouted behind her. Olwen was the daughter of the giant Ysbaddaden who refused to let her marry until the suitor Culhwch completed a serious of dangerous and near-impossible feats and tasks. The haiku does not actually depict this legendary figure, but a contemporary person called Olwen. Nevertheless, the poem conveys a sense of feminine grace and fragility. The silver moon pouring into the room corresponds with the lunar symbolism of the rabbit.

The Knocker's Bane

The tin miners freeze
at the low sound of knocking;
a sudden cave-in

Commentary

In Welsh and Cornish folklore, the Knockers are small creatures, either mischievous or benevolent, believed to inhabit tin mines. Their name comes from the characteristic sound of knocking on the mine walls that forebodes a cave-in. According to one theory, these little beings are the benevolent spirits of labourers who had died in previous accidents in tin mines. A Cornish folk belief says that they warn the miners of impending danger. For this reason, thoughtful workers leave small offerings to the Knockers, in thanksgiving for their warnings. These creatures are also known as *buccas*, though the latter are also encountered outside the mines.

The Fogou

The narrow chamber —
a little mouse eating grain
on a wintry night

Commentary

Fogous are underground, dry-stone chambers, found by archaeologists in some Iron Age and Romano-British settlements in Cornwall. They are usually up to 30 metres in length and 2 metres wide. These souterrains are made of buried stone walls that taper toward the top and are capped at the roof level using flat stone slabs. Their original purpose remains unknown, though it has been suggested that the *fogous* may have been hideouts in case of sudden raids. According to an alternative theory, these structures might have been used for food storage. The *fogous* bear a resemblance to souterrains constructed in Iron Age Scotland and early medieval Ireland.

Men of the Old North

Three hooded riders
roam across the steep moorlands
soaked in twilight mists

Commentary

Yr Hen Ogledd (meaning "the Old North"), is the Old Welsh term for a region of post-Roman northern Britain and southern Scotland, which was inhabited by Brythonic-speaking peoples. It included the significant kingdoms of Rheged, Alt Clut, Gododdin, and Elmet, as well as some other minor states and chiefdoms. *Bonedd Gwŷr y Gogledd* ("The Descent of the Men of the North") is a genealogical tract written in Middle Welsh, which traces the pedigrees of sixth-century Northern British rulers to a common ancestor, Coel Hen. The haiku poem above depicts three mounted scouts from the kingdom of Rheged riding across the moorland landscape of the North Pennines.

Caer Ligualid

Black ravens circling
above the mighty rampart
of an old fortress

Commentary

Caer Ligualid is the Old Welsh name for the present-day city of Carlisle in Cumbria, which was known in Roman times as *Luguvalium* ("the fort of Lugh's strength"). In the late 6th century, the settlement was presumably the court of Urien, the king of Rheged. Arms attributed to Urien in the Middle Ages featured a raven. According to Bede the Venerable, who described Saint Cuthbert's visit to Caer Ligualid, the town had a still-functioning aqueduct and impressive Roman walls in the 7th century. The haiku above was inspired by a famous passage from *Y Gododdin*, early medieval Welsh poem: "he fed black ravens on the rampart of a fortress, though he was no Arthur".

The Battle of Argoed Llwyfain

Saturday morning —
speartips hidden in the cloud
on a wooded hill

Commentary

Argoed Llwyfain ("before the elm wood") was the site of a great battle between Urien, the monarch of the Brythonic kingdom of Rheged, and Theodric (nicknamed *Fflamddwyn*, "the flame bearer") of the Anglian kingdom of Bernicia. The battle, victorious for Britons, was immortalised by the bard Taliesin in the early Welsh poem *Gwaith Argoed Llwyfain*.

Selcovia

Hunters trudge through snow
following the trail of blood
in the twilit woods

Commentary

The Selgovae were an Iron Age Celtic people who inhabited the southern part of Scotland, between the shires of Kirkcudbright and Dumfries. According to one theory, their name means "the hunters". The Selcovian huntsmen portrayed in the haiku are stalking a wounded deer. One of them is carrying a crossbow. The historical evidence for such representation comes from several early medieval Pictish stones which depict a crossbow as a hunting weapon. On the Drosten Stone, dated to the 9th century, a hooded hunter is shown crouched and firing his crossbow at an approaching boar. This type of weapon would be ideal for lying concealed in wait for the game since it would require less strength, less space and less movement to fire than a conventional bow.

Gododdin

Brooch-adorned warlords
feasting in the hilltop court;
baleful crows cawing

Commentary

In the post-Roman period, Gododdin (Old Welsh *Guotodin*) was a Brythonic kingdom in south-east Scotland. The name derives from the Votadini, an earlier tribal group which lived in the same region. The deeds of the men of Gododdin are praised in *Y Gododdin*, an early medieval Welsh epic poem describing the Battle of Catraeth, which was fought (around 600 CE) between them and the Angles of Bernicia and Deira. After a year of feasting at Din Eydin (present-day Edinburgh), the men of Gododdin assembled a host and rode to face the Angles. The Britons were utterly crushed, and out of all the warriors who went to Catraeth, the only one who returned alive was the bard Aneirin, who composed the elegiac poem in question. The haiku poem above conveys a sense of impending doom surrounding the feasting men of Gododdin.

Traprain Law

Wind in ponies' manes —
shafts of sunlight peering through
fleeting, steel-grey clouds

Commentary

Traprain Law is an Iron Age *oppidum* (hillfort) in East Lothian, Scotland. It is believed to be one of the major settlements of the Votadini people. In 1919, archaeologists discovered a large hoard of silver from the Roman era at the site. A few centuries later, Traprain Law was one of the strongholds of the kingdom of Gododdin, the descendants of the Votadini. Today, visitors to the hill can see small herds of Exmoor ponies – a rare breed of semi-feral horses.

Merlin Sylvestris

A long-haired hermit
sits still in the dense thicket;
a boar walks past him

Commentary

It is believed that after the disastrous battle of Arfderydd (fought in 573 between different Northern Brythonic factions), in which king Gwenddoleu ap Ceidio had been defeated and killed, his bard Myrddin Wyllt ("Merlin the Wild") went mad and fled into the Caledonian Forest, where he lived as a hermit. Myrddin is sometimes identified with Merlin the Wizard from Arthurian legends. According to the French metaphysician René Guénon, the wild boar and bear symbolized, respectively, the representatives of spiritual authority (Merlin or the druids) and temporal power (Arthur or the knights) among the ancient Celts. In myths and folklore, the opposition between the two animals refers to the primordial conflict between the clergy and royalty.

Alt Clut

A chain of beacons
lights up the colossal rock
in the grim gloaming

Commentary

Alt Clut ("Rock of the Clyde") was the Brythonic name for Dumbarton Rock, a stronghold on the north bank of the River Clyde in Scotland. It became a metonym for the early medieval kingdom of Alt Clut, which was known in later ages as Strathclyde.

Dunadd

Coronation rites —
snow on the young king's fair hair
gleams in the red dusk

Commentary

Dunadd ("fort on the River Add") is an Iron Age and early medieval hillfort in Argyll, Scotland. It is believed to have been the royal fortress and the capital of the Gaelic kingdom of Dál Riata. On the top of the hill, there is a footprint in a stone slab, which was presumably used in the coronation ceremonies of the Dál Riata kings. In the early medieval period, Dál Riata was one of the major forces in the Scottish geopolitical landscape. In the 9th century, it merged with the Pictish kingdom of Fortriu, although it is disputed whether it was a Pictish takeover of Dál Riata, or the other way around. In any case, this event laid the foundations for the future Kingdom of Alba.

Caledonia

The sound of carnyx
above the painted army
marching through the heath

Commentary

Caledonia was the Latin name given by the Romans to the regions beyond the northern frontier of the province Britannia. By the time of Roman conquest, Caledonia was inhabited by an amalgamation of Brythonic and Pictish tribes. In later ages, it was a name used to describe Scotland as a whole. The carnyx was a large trumpet, usually made of bronze and brass and shaped like an animal head. It was widely used in the Iron Age Celtic world, mainly for military purposes. Due to the thunderous and harsh sounds they made, carnyces were used to raise the army's morale and to intimidate enemies.

The haiku poem above depicts the Caledonian army, led by Calgacus (his name meaning "the Swordsman"), marching southwards to meet its Roman foes. According to the Roman historian Tacitus, the Caledonians suffered a disastrous defeat in the battle of Mons Graupius, which took place about 83 CE.

The Caoineag

A grievous keening
at the hazy waterfall;
the clock strikes midnight

Commentary

In Scottish folklore, the *caoineag* is a type of female spirit (similar to a *banshee*) who haunts secluded waterfalls, streams, and glens. She would wail and weep at night when someone's death was about to occur.

Beinn Nibheis

Rosy, fluffy clouds
float over the snow-capped peak;
the buzzard's shrill cry

Commentary

Beinn Nibheis, also known by its anglicised named Ben Nevis, is the highest mountain in the British Isles. The peak is located in the Scottish Highlands, near the town of Fort William. In Scottish Gaelic, *beinn* means "peak"; the etymology of *nibheis* is unknown, though it has been linked to "heavens" or "clouds".

Hebridean Harpist

Slowly burning peats
cast light on the bard's fingers
dancing on the strings

Commentary

The earliest depictions of a triangular-framed Celtic harp (*crott*) can be seen on 8th-century Pictish stone carvings. According to one theory, the Celtic harp originated in early medieval Scotland, and then spread throughout the British Isles. Traditionally, peat has been the most important fuel source in the Outer Hebrides, an island chain off the west coast of mainland Scotland.

The haiku poem above depicts a local harpist entertaining a Pictish overlord who is inspecting this remote part of his kingdom. It has been suggested that before the arrival of Norse settlers in the 9th century, the Outer Hebrides were culturally and linguistically Pictish. In contrast, the inhabitants of the Inner Hebrides had tighter bonds with the Gaelic kingdom of Dál Riata.

Newgrange

A beam of warm light
illuminates the chamber;
the long trumpet roars

Commentary

Newgrange is a Neolithic grand passage tomb, located in County Meath, Ireland. The monument, built around 3200 BCE, is famous for being aligned with the Winter Solstice sunrise, when the sun lights up the passage and chamber for approximately 17 minutes. This particular moment may have been a part of a religious ceremony. Though its details remain unknown to us, the haiku poem above connects this ritual with celebrating the return of the Sun and bidding farewell to the spirits of winter.

Archaeologists have uncovered more than one hundred Irish bronze horns. These wind instruments, dated from the Bronze Age to the early medieval period, are found in a variety of shapes and sizes. They were either side-blown or end-blown.

Glendalough

The faint chime of bells
across the silent valley
cloaked in snow and frost

Commentary

Glendalough (Irish: *Gleann Dá Loch*, meaning "Valley of two lakes") is a glacial valley in County Wicklow, Ireland. The site is famous for its early medieval monastic monuments, including several churches, stone crosses, and round tower. The first abbot of Glendalough was Saint Kevin, who lived in the 6th century. The haiku poem above conveys a sense of tranquillity during an early winter morning in Glendalough.

The round tower on the site is about 30 metres high, with an entrance 3.5 metres from the base. The building originally had six timber floors, accessible by ladders. The four floors above entrance level are each lit by a small window; while the top floor has four windows facing the cardinal compass points. The purpose of round towers is not clear, though it has been suggested that besides serving the function of belfries, they may have been store-houses or places of refuge in the case of sudden Viking raids.

Dún Aonghasa

She gazes sunwards,
far beyond mountainous waves;
tears merge with the sea

Commentary

Dún Aonghasa is a prehistoric promontory fort located on the Aran Islands off the west coast of Ireland. The fortress, built on the top of a rocky cliff towering above the sea, consists of four concentric, dry stone walls. It is surrounded by defensive stones (*chevaux de frise*) located outside of the middle wall of *Dún Aonghasa*. The fort had been inhabited since at least 1100 BCE. Those interested in learning more about the site and its curious history can read *A Study of the Fort of Dun Aengusa* written by the famous Irish antiquarian T. J. Westropp.

The Song of Amergin

Ferocious blizzard —
a forsaken Celtic harp
muffles the harsh wind

Commentary

Amergin, also known as Amairgen Glúingel ("Amairgen white knee"), was a druid and bard, one of the seven sons of Míl who took part in the Milesian conquest of Ireland from the Tuatha Dé Danann. The Milesians agreed to retreat back to the ocean beyond the ninth wave that was considered to be a magical boundary. They sailed towards the beach once signalled; however, the druids of the Tuatha Dé Danann used magic to create a storm which prevented them from reaching the shore. Amergin sang an invocation that called up the spirit of Ireland, which parted the storm and allowed the ship to land safely. This invocation has come to be known as *The Song of Amergin*.

The Grianan of Aileach

The ancient ringfort
emerges from a dense fog;
pale gold on the walls

Commentary

The Grianan of Aileach (Irish: *Grianán Ailigh*, meaning "the temple of the sun") is a triple-walled Iron Age ringfort located in County Donegal, Ireland. The main structure of the fort is thought to have been built in the early medieval period, although the archaeological evidence shows that the hill had been inhabited long before. Its circular walls are 4.5 metres thick and 5 metres high. According to Irish mythology and folklore, however, the fort was originally built by the Dagda, who is one of the principal deities in the ancient Irish pantheon.

The Paps of Anu

Patches of pale light
blend with crepuscular shades
amid breast-shaped peaks

Commentary

The Paps of Anu (Irish: *Dá Chích Anann*) are a pair of breast-shaped mountains in County Kerry, Ireland. They are named after Anu, the ancient Irish mother goddess, who is often likened to Danu, a legendary ancestral figure of the Tuatha Dé Danann. On top of each of the peaks are prehistoric cairns, which create an illusion of nipples capping the breasts.

Moonrise at Ben Bulben

December moonlight
on the frost-covered tombstone;
the poet's name glows

Commentary

Ben Bulben (Irish *Binn Ghulbain*) is a large limestone rock formation in County Sligo, Ireland. The mountain, associated with numerous old legends, also served as inspiration for William Butler Yeats, who was an Irish poet, playwright and folklorist. His grave is located in Drumcliffe Churchyard, in the shadow of Ben Bulben.

Luchta's Blessing

Triumphant war-cries
above the duskening glen —
unbroken shield wall

Luchta's Bane

A trickle of blood
splattered on unfinished shields;
dawn in the workshop

Commentary

In Irish mythology, Luchta (or Luchtaine) was the carpenter of the Tuatha Dé Danann. Along with his two brothers, Goibniu and Credne, he forms the divine triad of artisans. He was particularly known for his skill in making spear shafts and shields, which he crafted for gods participating in the Second Battle of Moytura. The haiku poems above illustrate the dual nature of the deity. On the one hand, Luchta bestows his blessings upon his militant devotees by making their shields hard and resistant to enemy blows. On the other hand, he is capable of thwarting a carpenter's work and causing accidents in workshops.

Credne

Hafts of faint sunlight
at the shield on the lake bed;
its bronze boss glitters

Commentary

In Irish mythology, Credne (or Creidhne) was the goldsmith and the bronzeworker of the Tuatha Dé Danann. Along with his two brothers, Goibniu and Luchta, he forms the divine triad of artisans. He was particularly known for his skill in making spear rivets, sword hilts, and shields bosses, which he made for gods participating in the Second Battle of Moytura. Furthermore, according to legend it was Credne who made King Nuada's silver hand, together with the divine physician Dian Cecht. The haiku poem above depicts a votive offering to Credne. The ancient Celts often deposited artefacts of high value into rivers, lakes, and bogs in order to gain the favour of deities.

Eithne

Streams of dappled light
pouring on her golden braids;
penumbral tower

Commentary

Eithne (or Ethniu) was the daughter of the Fomorian tyrant Balor and mother of Lugh. According to legend, she was imprisoned in a shining tower of glass on Tory Island (*Tór Mór* in Old Irish, which means "the high tower") because her father wanted to avoid a druid's prophecy which said he would be killed by his own grandson. Twelve women were assigned to guard Eithne and keep her in isolation in order to prevent men from reaching the tower. Eventually, Eithne was seduced by Cían, who had broken into the tower with the help of a druidess called Biróg. The imprisoned princess gave birth to Lugh, the slayer of Balor.

Fionnuala

A fair-haired princess
gazes at the lonely swan;
she closes her eyes

Commentary

In Irish mythology, Fionnuala (or Finnguala) was the daughter of the god Lir of the Tuatha Dé Danann. According to legend of the *Children of Lir*, she was cursed by her stepmother Aoife and transformed into a swan for a period of 900 years. Fionnuala is considered a tutelary deity of many lakes and rivers of Ireland.

PART TWO

GERMANIC HERITAGE

Dagr

Amid misty pines
streams of early dawn sunlight;
the campfire smoke glows

Commentary

In Norse mythology, Dagr is the divine personification of day and a companion of Nótt. Dagr's horse is called Skinfaxi ("the shining mane") whose golden glow lights up the Earth daily. Odin sent Dagr and Nótt into the sky in horse-drawn chariots to ride around the world. They create darkness and light, as one follows the other through the heavens. The haiku poem above depicts an early morning in a pine forest somewhere in Scandinavia. The brilliant rays of the rising sun penetrate through the dense woodland, illuminating the hunters' encampment, which is shrouded in a veil of thick mist and smoke.

Nótt

In the starlit fields —
faint echoes of howling wolves
carried by the wind

Commentary

In Norse mythology, Nótt is the divine personification of night, a companion of Dagr. Nótt's horse is called Hrímfaxi ("the frost mane"), who lets drops of foam fall from his bit which form the dew on the surface of the Earth. Odin sent Dagr and Nótt into the sky in horse-drawn chariots to ride around the world. They create darkness and light, as one follows the other through the heavens. The haiku poem above was inspired by *The Lone Wolf*, one of the most famous paintings by Alfred Wierusz-Kowalski. Wierusz-Kowalski was a 19th-century Polish painter best-known for his evocative depictions of rural life in winter.

I Took Up The Runes

The empty noose hangs
from a lonely windswept tree
as the evening falls

Hangaguð

The lifeless face falls
from a lonely windswept tree
as the new dawn fades

Commentary

Rúnatal (Odin's Rune Song), a section of the *Hávamál* (the most famous collection of Old Norse poetry), describes the god Odin's self-sacrifice on a windswept tree. In order to learn the secrets of the runes, Odin pierced his side with his dwarven spear Gungnir and then hung, without food or drink, for nine long days and nights on a tree (which is assumed to be Yggdrasil, the World Tree). The empty noose in the first poem suggests that the deity has left the temporal world in his shamanic soul-journey in the pursuit of hermetic knowledge and wisdom.

Hangaguð, which means "god of the hanged", is one of Odin's many names. It refers to his self-sacrifice on the windswept tree. The second poem depicts Odin's return from his shamanic soul-journey.

Grímnir

A hooded rambler
strides across the barren plains
in the falling sleet

Commentary

In Norse mythology, *Grímnir*, which means "the masked one", is one of Odin's many names. It is a well-known fact that Odin sometimes visits Midgard (the terrestrial world) in the guise of a hooded rambler or an old man.

Urðr

A purse with gold coins
laying on a cobwebbed shelf
in the locked cellar

Verðandi

A Dane's bearded axe
cracks open the willow shield;
a huge gush of blood

Skuld

A small child is born
on a stormy brumal night;
a sudden draught comes

Commentary

In Norse mythology, the Norns are three female beings who rule the destiny of gods and men. Urðr represented the past, Verðandi concerned herself with the present, whereas Skuld governed the future. Some Old Norse sagas depict them weaving the web of fate. The Norns sit by a well called Urðarbrunnr (meaning "Urðr's Well"), which is located beneath the world tree Yggdrasil.

The haiku poems above connect the tripartite concept of time with these mythical beings. Skuld was said to visit each newly born child to allot his or her future – the sudden draught in the third poem alludes to her arrival in the household. The adjective *brumal* means "pertaining to winter" or "winter-like".

Ratatoskr

A nimble squirrel
climbs up the moonlit ash tree;
the gnawing teeth glint

Commentary

In Norse mythology, Ratatoskr (Old Norse "drill-tooth") is a squirrel that scampers up and down the World Tree, Yggdrasil. The animal carries messages and "slanderous" gossips between the eagle in the topmost branches and the serpent Níðhöggr, who dwells beneath one of the three roots of the tree. According to Hilda Ellis Davidson, a distinguished scholar in the field of Norse mythology and folklore, "Yggdrasil was said to grow and to be destroyed continually, as living creatures of the mythological world, hart, goat and squirrel, gnawed at it". The haiku poem above depicts Ratatoskr climbing up Yggdrasil as the moonlight shines on the squirrel's teeth.

Mímisbrunnr

Beneath the deep roots —
a reflection of the sky
in the frozen eye

Commentary

In Norse mythology, Mímisbrunnr (Old Norse "Mímir's Well") is a well of wisdom and knowledge located beneath one of three roots of the world tree Yggdrasil. Mímir, the guardian and owner of the well, drinks mead daily from it. Odin sacrificed one of his eyes to the well in exchange for gaining profound wisdom and foresight. He became wistful and grievous, for he had suddenly become fully aware of the ephemeral phenomena happening in the world: the primordial cycles of birth, growth, and death.

Fehu I

A mirthful laughter
in the warmth of the mead-hall;
the new jarl's great feast

Fehu II

The fire consumes
the blood-soaked feasting table
where severed heads lay

Commentary

Fehu is the first rune of the Elder Futhark runic alphabet, meaning "(mobile) wealth". Fehu represents abundance, prosperity, income, luck, cattle, and harmony. Yet, according to the Old Icelandic runic poem:

"Wealth is a source of discord amongst kin
and fire of the sea
and path of the serpent"

The haiku poems above illustrate two different aspects of the rune. On the one hand, Fehu can bestow material prosperity and peace upon righteous ones. On the other hand, the very nature of wealth can be a source of discord, animosity, and misery.

Uruz

The sound of the lurs
breaks the silence on the moors;
the auroch's fierce roar

Commentary

Uruz is the second rune in the Elder Futhark runic alphabet, meaning "wild ox" or "water". Uruz represents fierceness, brute physical strength, speed, domination, vitality, determination, endurance, masculine potency, as well as sudden changes. Lur is a long bronze trumpet known from the Nordic Bronze Age. Archaeologists have uncovered numerous lurs in Scandinavia and Northern Germany.

Gebo I

The lovers exchange
a long, passionate embrace
to stay warm at night

Gebo II

An old wanderer
knocks hastily at the door;
a flash of the knife

Commentary

Gebo is the seventh rune in the Elder Futhark runic alphabet, meaning "gift". Gebo represents generosity, hospitality, sacrifice, and exchanges on all levels – including contracts, personal relationships, and partnerships. The haiku poems above illustrate two different aspects of the rune. On the one hand, it is essential to cultivate the virtues of generosity, kindness, and empathy within us. However, we have to be wary of wicked individuals who can take advantage of our altruism or hospitality. The second poem depicts an assassin or a burglar, who disguises himself as an old vagrant seeking shelter.

Isaz

The hypnotic gaze
on the plains of white stillness;
the iron swords clash

Commentary

Isaz is the eleventh rune in the Elder Futhark runic alphabet, meaning "ice". Isaz represents stillness, silence, self-preservation, inertia, lack of movement, frustration, as well as the concept of antimatter. The haiku poem above depicts a duel between two Viking warriors, whose swords clash in a climactic moment of stillness. In early medieval Scandinavia, *holmgang* was a ritualistic type of duel conducted in order to settle offences, arguments, and legal disputes. The combatants fought inside a pre-defined enclosure (usually within stone circles or a small island). If a man did not show up for the duel, the other belligerent was proclaimed to be the winner. In this case, the person who proposed the challenge would be labelled a *nidingr* (implying that the individual had lost their honour, or was a villain). In extreme cases, a *nidingr* could be ostracised and become exiled. A more capable warrior could volunteer to fight in the place of a weaker, outmatched friend.

Skaði's Blessing

Unforeseen rumble —
the avalanche passes by
two ladies skiing

Skaði's Bane

Snowdrift soaked in blood;
a hunter's frozen body
torn apart by wolves

Commentary

In Norse mythology, Skaði is a female deity associated with winter, hunting, archery, and skiing. The myths portray her as the daughter of a giant called Þjazi. Skaði is the wife of Njörðr, the god of the seas, seafaring, wind, and crop fertility. They fall out with each other regarding where they should live – Skaði would like to live in the mountains in her abode called *Þrymheimr*. Njörðr, however, prefers the sea.

The haiku poems above illustrate two different aspects of the goddess. On the one hand, she protects her devotees from avalanches, hypothermia, predators, and other life-threatening conditions or situations related to winter and mountains. On the other hand, Skaði possesses the power to take someone's life or health away, as the instance of the unfortunate hunter above illustrates.

Njörðr's Bane

After raging storm
full moon on the icy sea;
a forlorn drakkar

Njörðr's Blessing

December morning —
pale apricity lights up
the seafarer's face

Commentary

In Norse mythology, Njörðr is a deity associated with the seas, seafarers, fishing, wind and crop fertility. He lives in the heavens in a place called *Nóatún* ("ship-enclosure"). In some scholarly interpretations, he is connected with the earlier Germanic goddess Nerthus described by the Roman historian Tacitus in his work *Germania*. Njörðr is the husband of Skaði, the goddess of winter and mountains. They fall out with each other regarding where they should live – Skaði would like to live in the mountains in her abode called *Þrymheimr*. Njörðr, however, prefers the sea.

Drakkar was a type of longship used by the Vikings. This marine vessel had a single sail and mast (which were detachable – such design allowed better manoeuvrability) and was fitted with oars that the sailors used to propel the ship forward. The hull was constructed to be flexible so that it would move with the waves instead of against them. The head of a dragon, snake, horse, or swan was usually carved onto the bow. The Vikings also attached their shields along the side of the ship to have them ready in the event of an attack.

The haiku poems above illustrate the dual nature of Njörðr. As is often the case with water deities, they have the power to cause dangerous storms as well as create favourable weather conditions.

Vidar's Blessing

No sound of the wind
in the snowy pine forest;
the sun is setting

Vidar's Bane

The gathered crowd cheers
as his hot tongue is pulled out;
the convict's mute scream

Commentary

In Norse mythology, Vidar (Old Norse "wide ruler") is the son of Odin
and the giantess Gríðr. He was the god associated with vengeance, silence,
and stealth. Vidar possessed tremendous strength, which was only
surpassed by Thor. It is foretold that at Ragnarok he will slay the wolf
Fenrir, the devourer of Odin. Vidar will place one foot on the lower jaw of
the beast and seize its upper jaw in one hand, thus tearing Fenrir's mouth
apart and eventually avenging Odin. According to the Old Norse poem
Grímnismál, Vidar's residence (*Landvidi*) is described as a peaceful
woodland glade. The haiku poems above illustrate two different aspects of
the deity. On the one hand, Vidar bestows silence and tranquillity upon his
devotees and places associated with him (such as forests and woodland
glades). On the other hand, Vidar's vengeful nature enables him to inflict
muteness upon those who misuse the gift of speech – liars and
blasphemers.

Freyja

The Marian shrine —
the footsteps of the wild cat
upon the fresh snow

Commentary

In Norse mythology, Freyja is a goddess associated with love and fertility. Freyja's abode in Asgard was called *Fólkvangr* – a beautiful meadow, where, according to Norse beliefs, half of those who die in battle are taken to upon death. The goddess owned a chariot drawn by boars and another chariot pulled by two grey or black cats. According to some scholars, Frigg and Freyja may have been a single goddess. In some parts of central and northern Europe, the advent of the Christian religion replaced the cult of Freyja (or similar goddesses) with that of the Virgin Mary. The wild cat in the haiku above symbolizes Freyja, whose deep and primordial connection with Germanic folk has not been completely eradicated by Christianisation.

Frigg

In the high castle
she sits by the spinning wheel;
the threads of clouds form

Commentary

In Norse mythology, Frigg is the wife of Odin. Frigg is often depicted as being very beautiful, wearing a girdle hung with household keys, and weaving clouds on her spinning wheel. According to some scholars, Frigg and Freyja may have been a single goddess.

Ymir

An icy boulder
falls into the deep ravine;
a thunderous crash

Commentary

In Norse mythology, Ymir was the legendary progenitor of all giants. This primaeval being was brought into being when the fire of Muspelheim melted the ice of Niflheim. It is said that the three gods – Odin, Vili, and Ve – dragged Ymir's dead body to Ginnungagap (the primordial void), and there they set about creating the world. They made the earth from his flesh, oceans from his blood, mountains and hills from his bones, trees from his hair, and rocks and boulders from his teeth.

Hræsvelgr

The roar of the wind
cutting through the glacier
locked in permafrost

Commentary

In Norse mythology, Hræsvelgr (Old Norse "Corpse Swallower") is a giant who takes the shape of an eagle sitting at the edge of heaven. When he flaps his wings in flight, he creates a movement of air so strong that it causes the wind to blow in the terrestrial world.

Gjallarhorn

Cracks on the thick ice
spread as the glacier trembles;
twilight at the heights

Commentary

In Norse mythology, Gjallarhorn ("the yelling horn") is a long trumpet horn of the god Heimdallr. Its loud blast can be heard throughout all the Nine Worlds. It is foretold that at Ragnarok, the end of the world, Heimdallr will blow into Gjallarhorn in order to summon the gods to the final battle. Gjallarhorn is usually depicted as a lur, a long bronze trumpet known from the Nordic Bronze Age. Archaeologists have uncovered numerous lurs in Scandinavia and Northern Germany.

Róta

Her aureate braids
swing freely in the harsh wind;
the corpses vanish

Commentary

In Norse mythology, Róta is one of the valkyries. Valkyries (Old Norse "the choosers of the slain") are warrior-maidens of the god Odin who select men doomed to die in battle, and take take them to Valhalla (Old Norse "the hall of the slain"). Róta is depicted as a fair woman with a "snow-pale head".

Göndul and Skögul

Two horseback maidens
gaze at the desolate field
as the first snow falls

Commentary

In Norse mythology, Göndul and Skögul are a pair of the valkyries. Valkyries (Old Norse "the choosers of the slain") are warrior-maidens of the god Odin who select men doomed to die in battle, and take them to Valhalla, the hall of the slain. Göndul (Old Norse "wand-wielder") and Skögul (Old Norse "high-towering") are depicted as sitting "high-hearted on horseback", wearing helmets, and carrying shields.

Galdr

The waves rise and fall
as the fair sorceress sings
in the midnight air

Commentary

Galdr is an Old Norse word meaning "witchcraft", "spell", or "incantation". The practice of *galdr* involved chanting sacred verses (with a strong emphasis on words and rhythm), especially for a protective effect. It was presumably connected with runic magic, which was performed in order to get the desired effect of each particular rune.

Draugr

Approaching midnight;
full moon on the ghastly face
outside the barrow

Commentary

In Norse mythology and folklore, the *draugr* (plural *draugar*) is the incorporate spirit of a dead person. The Norse sagas depict them as fearsome and mischievous creatures guarding the treasure buried with them in their burial chamber. Sometimes they would rise from their resting place and torment living beings, including farm animals and humans. They are said to possess enormous strength and shape-shifting abilities. In J.R.R. Tolkien's fantasy novel *The Lord of the Rings*, the Barrow-wights were wraith-like revenants, whose behaviour and outward appearance was inspired by the Norse *draugar*. Another modern depiction of these creatures can be found in the video game *The Elder Scrolls V: Skyrim*, in which the *draugar* are ferocious undead monsters inhabiting ancient burial sites.

Myling

A phantasmal child
follows the lone wanderer;
he looks back in fear

Commentary

In Scandinavian folklore, the *mylingar* are vengeful incarnations of the souls of abandoned, unwanted, or unbaptised children, who are usually victims of infanticide. They are forced to wander the earth and harass lone wanderers at night, in an attempt to leap onto their back. If they succeed, they are difficult to get rid of and demand to be carried to the nearest cemetery for a proper burial in hallowed ground.

Huldra

An eerie kulning
echoes back across the lake
towards the dark trees

Commentary

In Scandinavian folklore, huldra is a malevolent, seductive forest creature. Folk tales always portray her as exceptionally beautiful, with long blonde hair. It is said that huldras lure young unmarried men into the mountains, where they force them into marriage.

Kulning is a traditional, high-pitched herding call used in some parts of Scandinavia.

The Road to Hel

Two ashen figures
stare at the funeral pyre
adrift on the sea

Commentary

The Road to Hel: A Study of the Conception of the Dead in Old Norse Literature is the title of a book by Hilda Ellis Davidson, a distinguished scholar in the field of Norse mythology and folklore. The book is an academic study of the funerary traditions and the conception of the afterlife in the pre-Christian Scandinavia.

The haiku poem above was inspired by *The Funeral of a Viking*, a painting by Frank Dicksee. The painting is a dramatic depiction of a Viking being cremated on a ship pushed out to sea. The 10th-century Arab Muslim writer Ahmad ibn Fadlan described a similar ship burial which was conducted by Vikings living along the Volga River.

Borgund stavkirke

Their vacant gazes
fixed on the old, stone altar;
the forgotten runes

Commentary

Borgund Stave Church is a triple-nave stave church located in the village
of Borgund in western Norway. The temple was built between 1180 and
1250. It was dedicated to the Apostle Andrew. Several runic inscriptions
have been found inside the church.

Valfar

A sleeping Viking
beneath the massive snowdrift;
ravens croak hoarsely

Commentary

The poem refers to Terje "Valfar" Bakken, the founder of the Norwegian black Viking metal band Windir. On January 14, 2004, Valfar went for a hike towards his family's cabin in the mountains, but never reached it. He had been caught in a snowstorm and died from hypothermia. Valfar's body was found by the authorities three days later.

Kraken

The agonized scream
followed by deathly silence;
bubbles on the sea

Commentary

In Scandinavian folklore, the kraken is a legendary sea monster which is rumoured to haunt the seas between Norway and Greenland and attack passing ships. The Norse sagas depict the creature as a giant octopus, squid, or crab, whose enormous body is often mistaken by sailors for an island. Kraken sightings have been documented as far back as the 13th century. The haiku poem above depicts this marine beast stealthily tearing apart and devouring a sailor who happened to stand too close to the ship's port side.

Andvari's Curse

Gleams of golden light
in the old king's frenzied eyes
as the stronghold burns

Commentary

In Norse mythology, Andvari (Old Norse "careful one") is a dwarf, owner of the magical ring Andvaranaut. The ring had the power to attract gold and wealth. Loki, the trickster god, robbed Andvari of his hoard of gold, which included the magical ring. In revenge, the dwarf cursed the ring to bring misery to whoever possessed it. Loki gave the treasure to the magician Hreidmar in compensation for killing his son Otr. Eventually, Andvari's gold became the hoard guarded by the dragon Fafnir.

The haiku poem above depicts the catastrophic consequences of obtaining Andvari's ring. Reflections of golden light in the king's eyes refer to the treasures voraciously hoarded by him. Bewildered by the accursed glamour of gold, the ruler becomes possessed with wickedness and greed. This ultimately leads to his downfall – enemies successfully assault his stronghold and set fire to it.

Fafnir's Lair

Clouds of noxious fumes
amid golden chalices;
snow pours in and melts

Commentary

In Norse mythology, Fafnir was a dwarf, son of the magician Hreidmar and brother of Regin and Otr. After being affected by the bane of Andvari's ring and gold, he became greedy and evil, eventually turning into a dragon. Fafnir breathed noxious fumes into the land around him so that no one would attempt to steal his treasure. Eventually, he was slain by the hero Sigurd, who was Regin's foster-son.

The haiku poem above is a depiction of Fafnir's cavern. Because of the beast's flaming fumes, the temperature of the interior is so high that snow pouring in through the entrance immediately melts.

Gamla Uppsala

Before the dawn breaks
heavy fog enshrouds the mounds;
the owl's piercing cry

Commentary

Gamla Uppsala ("Old Uppsala") is a village located two miles northeast of the modern city of Uppsala in Sweden. Archaeological excavations in this area have revealed precious artefacts dating from the Bronze Age through the Roman period to the Viking Age. Gamla Uppsala is also famous for its three Royal Mounds dating back to the sixth century. The mounds were said to contain the remains of Swedish kings of the legendary Yngling dynasty.

The Danish Queen

A chalk, windswept cliff —
patches of golden sunlight
on her bronze necklace

Commentary

In the Nordic Bronze Age, the elite of the time were buried in burial mounds with fine works of bronze and gold artisanship, which included pieces of jewellery.

Veksø

Drops of heavy dew
on the ritual helmets
glisten in the sun

Commentary

Veksø (or Viksø) is a peat bog extraction site in Zealand, Denmark, where a pair of Bronze Age ceremonial horned helmets (dating to ca. 1100–900 BCE) was found in 1942. They may have been deposited in the bog as votive offerings in a religious ceremony. The helmets, almost identical in design, were made of tin-rich bronze with low-level impurities of lead, arsenic, antimony, nickel, and silver. They were decorated with bosses and adorned with eyes and beaks. The haiku poem above depicts these ornamental helmets laying on the dewy grass moments before they are deposited in the swamp.

Tomb Raiders

The large oak coffin
hurriedly carried away
in the wintry gale

Commentary

The haiku poem above refers to round barrows with oak coffins, characteristic of the Danish Bronze Age. These waterlogged burial sites, dated to about 1350 BCE, were often disturbed and devastated by tomb robbers.

Winter at the Sognefjord

Rosy morning light
on a tall, silent boulder
by the frozen fjord

Commentary

The haiku poem above is a literary depiction of *Winter at the Sognefjord*, a painting by the Norwegian artist Johan Christian Dahl from 1827. As an important representative of Norwegian Romanticism, Dahl was renowned for his paintings of landscapes in Scandinavia and Germany. In his art, he sought to convey the profundity and awe he felt before nature. Dahl was influenced by Caspar David Friedrich's style – the two artists became friends and close associates in 1818.

The Fall of Gaul

Deafening footsteps
on the vast plains of thick ice;
sunset on the Rhine

Commentary

On the last day of the year 406, a mixed horde of Germanic tribes (which included Vandals, Alans, and Suebi) poured across the Rhine River into Gaul. According to the 18th century historian Edward Gibbon, the river was most likely frozen at that time of the year, which made the crossing easier. The primary consequence of the invasion was the gradual collapse of Roman civic order in northern Gaul, which significantly contributed to the ultimate downfall of the Western Roman Empire. The haiku poem above illustrates the huge scale of this crossing.

Hengest and Horsa

Dawn at Newbury —
two wild horses in the mist
rush to the oak trees

Commentary

Hengest and Horsa were two legendary brothers, who were said to be leaders of the first Anglo-Saxon settlers in Britain. The Old English names Hengest and Horsa mean "stallion" and "horse", respectively. According to one scholarly interpretation, the legend originates from the myth of a divine pair of brothers, which was common in the Indo-European tradition. The divine twins, such as the Greek Dioscuri or the Vedic Ashvins, were depicted as youthful horsemen who possessed magical powers of healing.

The haiku poem above also refers to the construction of the Newbury Bypass in 1996, which was met with protests of environmental activists due to the mass felling of old trees. On one February morning, two wild horses loomed out of the mist and rushed to the oak trees, trying to "save" them from being cut down.

Grendel, the Shadow-Walker

The stench of dead stag
rotting on the frozen swamps;
watchful eyes widen

Heorot

Dim light of the hearth
shines on the sleeping faces;
the door hinges creak

Beowulf's Decision

His shivering legs
by the hot, bloody water;
a shrill hiss of drakes

Commentary

These haiku poems refer to *Beowulf,* an epic poem written in Old English, which is set in early medieval Scandinavia. Beowulf, a young prince of the Geats, comes to the aid of Hrothgar, the king of the Danes, whose mead hall of Heorot has been under attack by a troll-like monster from the swamps known as Grendel. During the night, Grendel sneaks into the hall and devours one of the sleeping men. He is eventually defeated by Beowulf who kills him with his bare hands. The following night, Grendel's mother attacks Heorot, in an attempt to avenge her son. In the morning, Beowulf finds her cavern at the bottom of a hot lake and kills her. Fifty years later, Beowulf slays a dragon, though the beast mortally wounds him. Beowulf's retainers cremate his body and erect a burial mound in his memory.

Eoforwic

Thatched, snow-covered roofs
glitter brightly at daybreak;
redwings soar sun-wise

Commentary

Eoforwic (folk etymology "wild-boar town") was the Old English name for the city of York. During the Roman occupation of Britain, it was the location of a legionary fortress known as *Eboracum*, and its name was ultimately derived from the Brythonic *Eburākon*, which means "yew tree place". Throughout the Anglo-Saxon period, York was an important royal and ecclesiastical centre in the kingdom of Northumbria. In November 886, the city was captured by the Great Heathen Army of Vikings, only to be retaken by Anglo-Saxons a century later.

Redwings are winter birds common to the region of Yorkshire.

Sunset on the River Ouse

Large flocks of fieldfares
feed on snow-clad holly shrubs;
the river turns red

Commentary

Fieldfares are large, colourful thrushes. During the coldest months of winter, it is common to see flocks of fieldfares hunting for holly and hawthorn berries. These birds inhabit bushy hedgerows near the River Ouse, which flows through North Yorkshire.

Streanæshalc

A lone white wolf howls
under the icy full moon
as the abbey burns

Commentary

Streanæshalc ("the bay of the lighthouse") was the Old English name
for the earliest settlement at Whitby, North Yorkshire. The first abbey at
Whitby was founded in 657 by Oswiu, the king of Northumbria. The
monastery flourished until the Danish Viking leaders Ivar the Boneless and
Ubba laid waste to it in a series of raids, which took place between 867 and
870.

The famous writer Bram Stoker derived the inspiration for his Gothic
horror novel *Dracula* from the majestic remains of Whitby Abbey and the
local legend about a white ghost of a lady who wanders among the shadowy
ruins of the monastery. According to the legend, the lady was bricked up
alive inside one of the walls. The haiku poem above connects the historical
account of the Viking raid with later literary fiction. In Bram Stoker's novel,
Count Dracula had the power to transform himself into a wolf.

Lindisfarena

Gathering twilight —
red clouds on the ice-bound sea
hiding monk's crushed skull

Commentary

The Holy Island of Lindisfarne (Old English: *Lindisfarena*) is a tidal island off the northeast coast of England. The priory of Lindisfarne was founded in circa 635 by Irish-born missionary Saint Aidan, who had been summoned from Iona off the west coast of Scotland to Northumbria at the request of King Oswald of Northumbria. In summer 793, the monastery at Lindisfarne was attacked and plundered by a raiding party of Norwegian Vikings. This event is considered to be the beginning of the Viking age. *The Anglo-Saxon Chronicle* records:

In this year fierce, foreboding omens came over the land of the Northumbrians, and the wretched people shook; there were excessive whirlwinds, lightning, and fiery dragons were seen flying in the sky. These signs were followed by great famine, and a little after those, that same year on 6th ides of January, the ravaging of wretched heathen men destroyed God's church at Lindisfarne.

The setting of the haiku above is one winter dusk, a few years after the Viking raid on Lindisfarne.

Ragnar Lothbrok's Grave

The pit with snake bones
whitens at the new day-spring;
December snowfall

Commentary

Ragnar Lothbrok (whose epithet Lothbrok means "shaggy-breeches")
was a semi-legendary Norse king and hero, who is said to have lived in the
9th century. He is the subject of several Old Norse sagas and poems.
During his unsuccessful attempt to conquer England, Ragnar Lothbrok was
captured by King Ælla of Northumbria and thrown into a pit full of
venomous snakes where he died in agony. *Krákumál*, a skaldic poem
composed in the 12th century, consists of a monologue in 29 stanzas of ten
lines each delivered by the dying Norse hero. The haiku poem above depicts
the aforementioned snake pit in winter, several years after Ragnar
Lothbrok's death.

Tomworðig

The scop tells his tale
to king Penda and his court;
tears on their faces

Commentary

Tomworðig ("an open meadow by the River Tame") was the Old English name for the town of Tamworth in Staffordshire, England. In the sub-Roman period, it was inhabited by people who called themselves the *Tomsaete*. During king Penda's reign in the first half of the 7th century, Tamworth was the royal centre and capital of the Anglo-Saxon kingdom of Mercia. Penda, the last heathen ruler of Mercia, was a powerful leader, whose deeds were overshadowed only by Offa, who reigned in the second half of the 8th century.

Scop was the Old English name for an oral poet, akin to the Old Norse *skald*. These wordsmiths were attached to royal courts, where they recited old legends, tales, and eulogical praise poems.

Lundenwic

The crescent moon shines
on the still banks of the Thames;
drakkars in the mist

Commentary

Lundenwic was an Old English name for London. In the 9th century, London was attacked by Vikings during numerous raids. In 871, the Great Heathen Army reached London and it is assumed that the Vikings camped within the old Roman walls during the winter of that year.

Drakkar was a type of longship used by the Vikings. This marine vessel had a single sail and mast (which were detachable – such design allowed better manoeuvrability), and was fitted with oars that the sailors used to propel the ship forward. The hull was constructed to be flexible so that it would move with the waves instead of against them. The head of a dragon, snake, horse, or swan was usually carved onto the bow. The Vikings also attached their shields along the side of the ship to have them ready in the event of an attack.

Uhtcearu

Flickering candle
lights up her lustreless face;
the storm rages on

Commentary

Uhtcearu is an Old English word referring to a feeling of anxiety or uneasiness before the dawn. The haiku poem above depicts a restless woman waiting for the homecoming of her husband.

Sutton Hoo

As the sun goes down
shadows creep onto the mounds
soaked in rosy rime

Commentary

Sutton Hoo is an important early medieval archaeological site near Woodbridge in Suffolk, eastern England. An Anglo-Saxon ship burial containing rich grave goods (which included the famous ornamental helmet), probably for the 7th-century East Anglian king Rædwald, was found there in 1939.

Valravn

The deadly arrow
pierces Sidrac's only eye;
a raven swoops down

Commentary

The haiku poem above refers to the Battle of Englefield, which took place around the 31st of December 870, at Englefield near Reading in Berkshire, England. It was a military conflict between the Saxons of Wessex and the Danish Vikings, victorious for the former. It was one of many back-and-forth armed skirmishes in the Danish invasion which almost ended Anglo-Saxon independence in England. *The Anglo-Saxon Chronicle* records:

This year came the [Danish] army to Reading in Wessex; and in the course of three nights after rode two earls up, who were met by Alderman Ethelwulf at Englefield; where he fought with them, and obtained the victory. There one of them was slain, whose name was Sidrac.

In Danish folklore, the *valravn* ("raven of the slain") is a mythical species of a raven which are said to consume the bodies of the dead on the battlefield. If they eat the corpse of a king or chieftain, they gain supernatural power and knowledge.

PART THREE

GREEK AND ROMAN HERITAGE

Persephone

Autumn fades away —
trickling rain merges with frost
on the mossy roof

Commentary

In ancient Greek mythology, Persephone was a daughter of Zeus and Demeter. Her Roman counterpart was known as Proserpine. According to the myth, she was gathering flowers on a meadow when suddenly the earth opened up and Hades abducted her. The god made Persephone his wife and queen of the netherworld. She was forced to spend the winter months there and allowed to return to the surface of the earth for the rest of the year. The myth of Persephone's disappearance symbolizes her function as the personification of vegetation, which shoots forth in spring and withdraws into the earth at autumn-time. The haiku poem above illustrates how the last days of autumn slowly and subtly make way for winter.

Chloris

November sunrise —
the scent of crimson roses
sprinkled with light frost

Commentary

In ancient Greek mythology, Chloris was the goddess of spring and flowers. She was said to have created the very first rose. While strolling through the woods one morning, Chloris found the lifeless body of a beautiful nymph. Motivated by pity and despair over the nymph's passing, she transformed her into a flower in order to preserve her fragile beauty. Chloris asked the Olympian gods for help: Aphrodite adorned the flower with beauty and Dionysus added nectar to give it a delightful fragrance. Zephyrus, the god of the West Wind, drove the clouds away so that Apollo, the sun god, could shine and make the rose bloom.

Psyche

In the dark cellar
a butterfly awakens
from its resting place

Commentary

In ancient Graeco-Roman mythology, Psyche was a princess of extraordinary grace and charm, whose beauty provoked the jealousy of Venus. She is the subject of a famous myth described in *The Metamorphoses*, written by Apuleius. According to Apuleius, the envious Venus ordered her son Cupid (the god of love, known in Greek mythology as Eros) to make Psyche fall in love with the most despicable of men. Disobeying his mother's request, Cupid placed Psyche in a remote place where he could come to her secretly and, by his warning, only in pitch-black darkness. Following the advice of her concerned sisters, one night Psyche lit a lamp and discovered that the figure at her side was Cupid himself. When a spill of hot oil from the lamp awakened him, the god of love immediately fled. Roaming the earth in search of him, Psyche was captured by Venus, who imposed demanding tasks upon her. Eventually, touched by Psyche's repentance, Cupid rescued her, and, at his instigation, Jupiter made her immortal and let her marry Cupid. In art, Psyche is often portrayed with butterfly wings. In ancient Greek mythology, the soul was depicted as a butterfly, which is another meaning of the word *psychē*.

Dodona

The priest's deep silence
as the snow falls on cauldrons;
the leafless oak tree

Commentary

In ancient Greek religion, Dodona was the oldest Hellenic oracle dedicated to Zeus and Dione. It was situated in Epirus, in a flat valley in the northwestern part of Greece. According to various accounts from Classical Antiquity, priestesses and priests in the sacred grove listened to the rustling of the oak leaves in order to determine the correct course of action. According to another interpretation, however, the oracular sound was made by bronze cauldrons suspended from oak branches (or set upon tripods surrounding the sacred trees). The bronze vessels sounded with the wind blowing in a manner similar to wind chimes.

Mount Olympus

The flushed afterglow
illuminates the high clouds
that obscure the throne

Commentary

Mount Olympus is the name of the abode of the Twelve Olympian Gods of the ancient Greek world. It is also the site of the throne of Zeus, the principal Olympian deity. According to myths, Mount Olympus was erected following the Titanomachy, the epic conflict between the young gods, the Olympians, and the older generation of gods, the Titans. Numerous peaks in the Hellenic world were named *Olympus*. However, according to classical sources, it is assumed that the very dwelling of the Olympian gods is at the Mount Olympus located on the border between Thessaly and Macedon, near the Aegean Sea.

Prometheus Bound

Desolate mountains —
the cold light of Jupiter
on a frail body

Commentary

In ancient Greek religion, Prometheus was one of the titans. According to the Greek poet Hesiod, Zeus, the principal Olympian god, had been duped by Prometheus into accepting a sacrifice that consisted of bones wrapped in fat instead of meat. The angered Zeus hid fire from humanity. Prometheus, however, stole it and brought it to Earth once again. In retribution, Zeus had the titan nailed to a remote mountain in the Caucasus and sent an eagle to devour his immortal liver, which regularly regenerated itself. The Greek playwright Aeschylus depicted Prometheus in his tragedy *Prometheus Bound*. The titan was not only portrayed as the bringer of fire and civilization to humankind. His function as its preserver and sustainer was also emphasized. The haiku poem above was inspired by a painting by Thomas Cole, which shows the cold light of Jupiter (the Roman equivalent of Zeus) shining on the giant's naked body.

Boreas

An empty pathway
high in the misty mountains;
wailing in the trees

Commentary

In ancient Greek religion, Boreas was the personification of the northern wind, one of the four seasonal *Anemoi* (deities of wind). He is also the god of winter who is said to descend from the cold mountains of Thrace, cooling the air with his icy breath. Beyond his mountain abode lays Hyperborea, the legendary land of eternal spring unaffected by the god's fierce winds. The Greek historian Herodotus relates how Boreas destroyed the naval army of the Persian king Xerxes off the beach Sepias in Thessaly, in order to show affection toward the Athenians. As a token of their gratitude, the Athenians built him a temple near the Ilissus and held a festival in his honour. Works of art portray Boreas as winged, bearded, and powerful; he often wears a short, pleated tunic.

Enkrateia

The drunken hoplites
laugh at their sober comrade
praying in silence

***

The Persian's arrow
misses the sleeping hoplite;
the archer's slit throat

Commentary

Enkrateia is an ancient Greek virtue, which is usually translated to "self-mastery" or "power over oneself". The setting of the haiku poems above is the night before a decisive battle between Athenians and Persians. In the first poem, a group of Greek hoplites decides to ease their fear of the upcoming conflict. Intoxicated with wine, they laugh at their comrade who prefers to stay sober and pray to Zeus instead. In the second poem, the drunken soldiers are asleep when the Persians conduct a surprise raid on the camp. One Persian archer draws his bow, in an attempt to kill one of the sleeping Athenians. However, he is stopped halfway, as the watchful abstinent hoplite stealthily slits his throat. Thanks to this one man's sobriety, the alarm is raised and the Persians fail to ambush the Greeks.

Anabasis

A snow-blind hoplite
perishes in the crevice;
dusk at the high pass

Commentary

Anabasis is the title of a book written by Xenophon, a Greek historian
and military leader. Xenophon joined the Ten Thousand, a large force of
Greek mercenaries hired by Cyrus the Younger, who wanted to seize the
throne of Persia from his brother, Artaxerxes II. Cyrus was killed at the
Battle of Cunaxa (401 BCE), rendering the actions of the Greeks irrelevant
and the campaign a failure. Anabasis contains a famous account of the
mercenaries' long retreat ("the march of the Ten Thousand") from near
Babylon to the Black Sea. It is said that Xenophon's resourcefulness and
bravery were mostly responsible for the success of their retreat.

The haiku poem above was inspired by Book 4, Chapter 5 of *Anabasis*,
which depicts the hardships of the Hellenic army in the snow-covered
mountains of Armenia:

"On the heels of the army hung perpetually bands of the enemy,
snatching away disabled baggage animals and fighting with each other over
the carcases. And in its track not seldom were left to their fate disabled
soldiers, struck down with snow-blindness or with toes mortified by
frostbite."

Megas Basileus

In the heat of fight
a dart pierces his corslet;
the scarlet-streaked sky

Commentary

Megas Basileus is a Greek term meaning "great king". The title was assumed by Alexander the Great and his Hellenistic successors. In the winter of 327 or 326 BCE, Alexander personally led a successful military expedition against the Aspasioi of the Kunar valley (located in present-day north-eastern Afghanistan). In a fierce battle, Alexander himself was wounded in the shoulder by a dart. The haiku poem above refers to this very moment. According to some scholars, Alexander the Great was deified in Egypt following his visit to the oracle of Ammon at Siwa in 331 BCE. The scarlet-streaked sky symbolizes the Macedonian's wound and refers to the traditional law of analogy, which emphasizes the correspondence between heaven and the earthly plane. In other words, what happens on one level of reality can also influence every other level. This sacred connection has been forgotten in the modern world, which labels such viewpoints as "superstitious". It was first formulated by Hermes Trismegistus in the *Emerald Tablet.*

"That which is Below corresponds to that which is Above, and that which is Above, corresponds to that which is Below, to accomplish the miracles of the One Thing."

Kleos

The old phalangite
spins a tale of Babylon;
campfire near the sea

Commentary

Kleos is a Greek word, often translated to "glory", "renown", or, more specifically, "what people say about you". *Kleos* is earned through achieving honourable deeds. The haiku poem above depicts a veteran Macedonian phalangite who tells the story of his adventures in Asia when he served in Alexander the Great's army.

Hecatomb

The sun is rising —
the smell of burning corpses
on the misty heights

Commentary

In ancient Greek and Roman religion, *hecatomb* had initially been a great feast and sacrifice of a hundred oxen. In later times, it referred to a large number of any animals slaughtered for sacrifice. In a metaphorical sense, *hecatomb* is used to describe the sacrifice or destruction by fire, storm, epidemic or sword of any significant number of people or animals. It can also allude to the destruction of inanimate objects or even annihilation of psychological and moral qualities.

Lycanthropy

An unearthly howl
in the Arcadian woods;
his moonlit turn-skin

Commentary

Lycanthropy is a name employed in folklore for the liability or power of a human being to transform into an animal, especially a wolf. There are numerous classical accounts of lycanthropy. For instance, the Greek historian Herodotus recorded that the Neuri, a tribe he located as living in the north-east of Scythia, underwent a metamorphosis into wolves once every year for several days, and then returned to their original human shape. In the 2nd century BCE, the Greek geographer Pausanias related the story of Lycaon, who was transformed into a wolf because he had been identified as the culprit of infanticide. Finally, the Roman poet Ovid describes men who roamed the woods of Arcadia in the form of wolves.

Polyphemus

The sheep and goat bones
in a dark, musty cavern;
the one-eyed beast sleeps

Commentary

In ancient Greek mythology, Polyphemus was the most famous of the Cyclopes, who are a race of one-eyed giants. He is the son of Poseidon, the god of the sea, and the nymph Thoösa. According to *The Odyssey*, when Odysseus was shipwrecked on the coast of Sicily, he was captured by Polyphemus. The Cyclope trapped him and twelve of his companions in a cave and blocked the entrance with a huge rock. Eventually, Odysseus succeeded in making Polyphemus drunk and blinded the sleeping giant by plunging a burning stick into his eye. Although six of Odysseus' crew members had already been devoured by Polyphemus, this allowed Odysseus and those still alive to escape by clinging to the underbellies of the Cyclope's sheep let out to graze.

Helen of Sparta

As she undresses
the icy moon slips into
the silver mirror

Commentary

In ancient Greek mythology, Helen of Sparta was the most beautiful woman in Greece and the indirect cause of the Trojan War. She was the daughter of Zeus and sibling of the Dioscuri. As a young girl, Helen was kidnapped by Theseus, only to be rescued by her brothers. She was also the sister of Clytemnestra, who became the wife of Agamemnon. Helen's suitors came from all over Greece, and from among them, she decided to marry Menelaus, Agamemnon's younger brother. While Menelaus was absent, however, Helen was abducted to Troy by Paris, son of the Trojan king Priam. When Philoctetes slew Paris, she married Deiphobus, whom she betrayed to Menelaus when the Achaeans subsequently captured Troy. In the end, Helen returned with Menelaus to Sparta, where they lived happily until their deaths.

Pitys

Fluffy white snowflakes
fall from the lonely fir tree;
the northern wind blows

Commentary

In ancient Greek mythology, Pitys was an Oread nymph who was pursued by Pan, the wild rustic god. She was transformed into a pine tree by the gods in order to escape him.

Akrasia

The rebuked children
continue to plot their prank
as their father leaves

Commentary

The Greek word *akrasia* is usually translated to 'lack of self-control', but it has come to be used as a generic term for the phenomenon known as weakness or incontinence of will, or the inclination to act contrary to one's considered judgment about what is best to do. The *akratic* person gives in to the irrational feeling rather than reason more often than the average person. The haiku poem above illustrates the flaw of *akrasia*. The father reprimands his children for their misconduct. Despite being admonished and shown that what they are planning is unreasonable and possibly dangerous, the children continue to frame their prank.

Eureka!

The weary shepherd
kneels by the icy ravine;
the bleat of the sheep

Commentary

The ancient Greek word *eureka* means "I have found" — it is an exclamation indicating sudden discovery. The haiku poem above depicts a shepherd who has just found this stray sheep.

Diana

In a hunting lodge
antlers glow in silver light;
freezing moon rises

Commentary

In ancient Roman religion, Diana was the goddess of wild animals, hunting, and the moon. Originally, Diana had been an indigenous Italian goddess of the woodlands, though later she began to be identified with the Greek goddess Artemis. Eventually, Diana's role extended into that of a lunar deity and a patron of women. Given her role as the protectress of childbirth, she was invoked by women to aid conception and labour. Roman art depicts Diana as a huntress with bow and quiver, accompanied by a hound or deer.

Trivia

A way-worn rover
hesitates at the crossroads;
the full moon appears

Commentary

In ancient Roman religion, Trivia was the goddess associated with crossroads and witchcraft. Sometimes she is perceived as another, darker aspect of the goddess Diana. Trivia's name derives from the Latin *trivium*, "triple way", and alludes to her tutelage over roadways, particularly Y-junctions and three-way crossroads. She is the equivalent of the ancient Greek goddess Hecate.

The haiku poem above depicts a weary wanderer travelling at night. Because of Trivia's blessing, the full moon (which is one of the primary symbols associated with this goddess) comes out and, figuratively speaking, illuminates the rover's mind, helping him choose the right way.

Venus

The stone face brightens
as the stream of soft starlight
fills the darkened shrine

Commentary

Venus had originally been an ancient Italian goddess associated with agriculture and gardens. She was later identified by the Romans with the Greek goddess of love, Aphrodite. The second planet away from the Sun was named after her. Venus, as a celestial body, is always approximately in the same direction in the sky as the Sun and can be seen only in the hours around dawn and dusk. When it is visible, it is the brightest planet in the sky. Venus was known in ancient Greece by two different names: *Phosphorus* when it appeared as a morning star and *Hesperus* in its evening appearance. Romans called the morning star *Lucifer*. The haiku poem above depicts how the soft light of Venus illuminates the dark shrine before the dawn.

The Lotus-Eaters

Rome is all ablaze
as the lavish feast begins;
blood meddles with wine

Commentary

In ancient Greek mythology, the *Lotophagoi* ("the Lotus-Eaters") was a tribe encountered by the Greek hero Odysseus during his homecoming from Troy. Some companions of Odysseus were invited by the *Lotophagoi* to taste the mysterious plant. Those who did so were overcome by languorous forgetfulness. They had to be dragged back to the ship by force and chained to the rowing-benches; they would never have returned to their duties, otherwise. In a figurative sense, the phrase "lotus-eater" is used to describe a person who leads a life of indolent forgetfulness and luxury, instead of dealing with practical concerns and tasks. The haiku poem above depicts the degeneracy of late Roman aristocrats, who indulged in pleasures of the senses instead of trying to repair the gradually collapsing empire.

Nemestrinus

The old olive grove —
the brilliant sunlight warms up
the snow-covered soil

Commentary

In ancient Roman religion, Nemestrinus was a minor god of groves. His name is connected with nemus, "wood."

Volturnus

Source of the Tiber —
an eagle soaring above
the tranquil beech woods

Commentary

In ancient Roman religion, Volturnus was an obscure deity of Etruscan origin, whose role remains uncertain. Classical scholar Theodor Mommsen believed that Volturnus was the cult name for the tutelary god of the Tiber river. Another theory suggests that he might have been an agricultural deity. According to one etymological explanation, his name derives from the verb *volvere*, which means "to roll along or wind around". The deity's festival, *Volturnalia*, was held on August 27.

The haiku poem above follows Mommsen's interpretation and depicts the source of the Tiber on Mount Fumaiolo in the Apennines. During the 1930s, Benito Mussolini placed an antique marble Roman column at the point where the river arises, inscribed QUI NASCE IL FIUME SACRO AI DESTINI DI ROMA ("Here is born the river sacred to the destinies of Rome"). There is an eagle on the top of this column.

Angerona

A stern-browed flamen
prays in the silent temple
as the weak sun sets

Commentary

In ancient Roman religion, Angerona was the goddess associated with silence. It is believed that Angerona, as the divine protectress of Rome, represented the secret magical name of the Eternal City, which was not to be spoken aloud. In artistic depictions, she has a bandaged mouth and a finger pressed to her lips in demand for silence. According to Georges Dumézil, she helps nature and people overcome the yearly crisis of the winter days. Therefore, Angerona was worshipped as the remover of anguish and pain caused by the lack of sunlight and the cold. Her festival (*Angeronalia* or *Divalia*) was observed on December 21. The haiku poem above depicts an anguished Roman priest (*flamen*) praying to Angerona on the Winter Solstice.

Temple of Carmenta

The cold marble floor —
a pregnant mother shivers
as she prays barefoot

Commentary

In ancient Roman religion, Carmenta (or Carmentis) was the goddess of childbirth, midwives, and prophecy. She is one of the four *Camenae*, the divine patronesses of pregnancy and delivery. Women often prayed to Carmenta in order to soothe the pains of labour. There was a ban on wearing leather or other forms of dead skin in her temple, which was located next to the *Porta Carmentalis* in Rome. It meant that Carmenta was to be approached barefoot. Her festival, called the *Carmentalia*, was observed on January 11 and January 15. The haiku poem above depicts a pregnant woman praying to Carmenta for a safe delivery.

Postverta's Bane

A weeping old man
enters the mausoleum;
slush on his worn shoes

Commentary

In ancient Roman religion, Postverta was the goddess of childbirth and the past. She is one of the four *Camenae*, the divine patronesses of pregnancy and delivery. The haiku poem above depicts a dejected and aggrieved elder who enters a mausoleum on the anniversary of his son's passing. The old man's offspring was born as a cripple and died shortly after delivery. Affected by Postverta's bane, children were denied to him and his wife. Roman funerary practices included placing the whole body in a sarcophagus or cremating it and then depositing the ashes in urns. However, the law prohibited burial within the confines of the city; thus, cemeteries and mausoleums were located beyond city walls.

Laverna's Blessing

A hiemal twilight —
two thieves shrink into shadows
as the watchman yawns

Commentary

In ancient Roman religion, Laverna was the goddess of the criminal underworld. She is a divine protectress of thieves, robbers, charlatans, counterfeiters, and dishonest merchants. Laverna's sanctuary was located on the Aventine Hill, near *Porta Lavernalis*, a gate named after her. She was originally an old Etruscan goddess associated with darkness and the spirits of the underworld. It is said that libations to Laverna were poured with the left hand. In many traditional cultures, the left hand has negative connotations with bad luck, malice or breaking taboos. In fact, the Latin adjective *sinistro* or *sinistra* means "left" as well as "unlucky". Many hermetic spiritual traditions speak of the Left-Hand Path, as opposed to the Right-Hand Path. Followers of the Left-Hand Path, such as the Vedic Tantrics, often question and reject some religious and moral dogmas, preferring an unorthodox approach to spirituality.

The haiku poem above depicts two thieves who take advantage of the watchman's drowsiness, which was caused by Laverna's auspicious blessing. The mischiefs evade being detected by slipping into the shadows of the growing dusk. The adjective *hiemal* derives from Latin *hiemālis* (meaning "pertaining to winter").

Cardea's Bane

The sound of snoring —
nimble fingers pick the lock
as the night wears on

Commentary

In ancient Roman religion, Cardea was the goddess of the door hinge and liminal spaces. She was worshipped as the protectress of the family and children of the household. Cardea was associated with two other deities who preside over doorways: Forculus ("door") and Limentinus ("threshold"). In Ovid's *Fasti*, Cardea's function is described as follows: "by means of her divine presence, she opens things that have been closed and closes things that have been opened".

The haiku poem above depicts a burglar breaking into a wealthy urban household. Simple padlocks have been used in Europe since at least 400 BCE, though more complex mechanical locks were designed by Roman engineers. Their invention was necessitated by the increasing number of upper-middle-class villas and the decline in the number of domestic servants.

Empanda's Blessing

A frostbitten tramp
carried to the warm temple;
the smell of mulled wine

Commentary

In ancient Roman religion, Empanda was the goddess of asylum, charity, and hospitality. Empanda's sanctuary was located near the *Porta Pandana*, a gate in the fortifications of the Capitoline Hill. It is said that her temple was always open to anyone who needed protection or shelter.

The haiku poem above is set on a cold winter night. A homeless person is saved from certain hypothermia by being taken into Empanda's sanctuary. The smell of mulled wine does not refer to the tramp's alcoholic breath, however. Instead, it suggests that he is given some warm, spiced wine so that he can recover from his prolonged exposure to frost. There is evidence that wine was heated in ancient Rome as far back as the 2nd century.

Lupercalia

The wolf-headed men emerge laughing from the cave; the pope's blazing face

Commentary

In ancient Roman religion, Lupercalia was a festival observed annually on February 15 under the direction of a congregation of priests called *Luperci* ("brothers of the wolf"). The roots of the festival are obscure, although it has been suggested that it originated from the worship of an ancient deity who defended herds from wolves. The celebration was also connected with the legendary she-wolf who nurtured Romulus and Remus, the mythical founders of Rome.

Lupercalia began with the sacrifice of goats and a dog by the *Luperci*. The offering took place in the Lupercal cave on Palatine Hill. Then, the Luperci cut thongs (*februa* – hence the name of the month February) from the skins of the slaughtered animals and ran naked or half-naked in two groups around Palatine Hill, hitting any woman who got in their way with thongs. It was believed that a blow from the thong was supposed to render a woman fertile. According to Pope Gelasius I, only the "vile rabble" took part in the Lupercalia. The pope wanted to suppress the festival; the Senate, however, protested as they believed that Lupercalia was crucial to Rome's safety and prosperity.

Pons Sublicius

Crippled vagabonds
hunch over the crackling fire —
cold wind bites their cheeks

Commentary

In ancient Rome, *Pons Sublicius* was the oldest and most famous of the bridges across the Tiber. According to legend, it was built by Ancus Martius around 642 BCE. This wooden bridge was a favourite resort for beggars, who used to sit upon it and demand alms.

The Battle of the Trebbia

The elephants charge
into the fierce hail of darts;
trunks in blood and snow

Commentary

The Battle of the Trebbia River was the first major battle of the Second Punic War, a military conflict between the Carthaginian Empire and the Roman Republic. It took place in December of 218 BCE, around the Winter Solstice. After Hannibal, the leader of the Carthaginian army, had successfully crossed the Alps, he met the Roman forces on the left bank of the Trebbia river. Some Celtic tribes of northern Italy also reinforced both sides. The battle resulted in a decisive victory of the Carthaginian army against the Roman legions which were commanded by Tiberius Sempronius Longus. The haiku poem above depicts the charge of Carthaginian elephants against the light Roman infantry (*velites*). The latter are trying to stop the animals with a volley of darts (*plumbatae*).

Terror cimbricus

The icy wind howls
in the deserted villa;
snow on headless busts

Commentary

The phrase *terror cimbricus* was used by ancient Romans in 105 BCE to describe the panic and state of emergency that ensued as they prepared for the invasion of the Cimbri, a Germanic tribe. Forced out of the Jutland peninsula by overpopulation and the flooding of their territories, the Cimbri migrated southwards. The Teutoni and other Germanic tribes joined them along their route. This barbarian confederacy defeated the Romans in a series of successful battles. Following a particularly disastrous Roman loss in 105 BCE at Arausio, command of the Roman legions was assumed by Gaius Marius, who had previously successfully campaigned against Jugurtha of Numidia. In 102 BCE Marius destroyed the Teutoni at Aquae Sextiae. A year later, he joined forces with Quintus Lutatius Catulus and annihilated the entire Cimbri army at Vercellae. The haiku poem above depicts a Roman villa in northern Italy that was deserted by its inhabitants in the wake of the Cimbrian invasion.

Alea iacta est

The fiery sunrise
paints the silent river red
as the trumpets roar

Commentary

Alea iacta est (meaning "The die is cast") is a Latin phrase attributed by Suetonius and Plutarch to Julius Caesar on January 10, 49 BCE. On this day, Caesar ordered his army to cross the Rubicon river in Northern Italy. With this step, he entered Italy against the laws of the Senate and started his long civil war against Pompey and the conservative faction of the Optimates. The phrase, either in the Latin original or in translation, is used to indicate that a situation is sure to develop in a particular manner because decisions have been made that cannot be altered.

Discordia

Small drops of warm blood
dribble from the *pugio*;
the Caesar's quick death

Commentary

In ancient Roman religion, Discordia was the goddess of strife, conflict, and discordance. She is similar to the Greek goddess Eris. Her opposite is Concordia. In Virgil's *Aeneid*, she is described as "lunatic Discordia", who appears in the retinue of Mars and Bellona, the principal war deities. Sometimes, she is also identified with the Greek Ate, the goddess of mischief (the daughter of Eris), whose favourite pastime is pitting both mortals and immortals against each other, making them do unwise things that they later regret.

The haiku poem above depicts the assassination of Julius Caesar, which took place on the Ides of March (15 March) of 44 BCE. The politician was stabbed with a *pugio* (plural: *pugiones*), which was a small dagger used in close-quarters combat. Because it could be easily concealed, it was the weapon of choice for assassinations and suicides. According to Cicero and Suetonius, the conspirators who killed Julius Caesar used *pugiones*. From a metaphysical perspective, the entire event was stirred by Discordia, similarly to how Eris caused the Trojan War.

Sol Invictus

A youthful horseman
arrives at the temple doors;
an icicle breaks

Commentary

In ancient Roman religion, Sol was the name of two distinct sun gods. The original Sol, or Sol Indiges, had a shrine on the Quirinal and another shrine in the Circus Maximus which he shared with the moon goddess, Luna. His annual festival was marked with a sacrifice on August 9. Although the cult of Sol seems to have been native to Italy, Roman poets equated him with the Greek sun-god Helios.

The worship of Sol assumed an entirely different character with the later introduction of various sun cults from Syria. The Roman emperor Elagabalus (who ruled 218–222 CE) erected a temple dedicated to Sol Invictus on the Palatine. He tried to make his cult the dominant religion of Rome. The emperor Aurelian (who ruled 270–275 CE) later restored the worship and raised a great temple to Sol in the Campus Agrippae. The cult of Sol as a special protector of the emperors and the Empire remained the principal imperial cult until Christianity replaced it.

Camboglanna

The scarlet dusk falls
as soldiers crouch round the fire;
a bullfinch lands near

Commentary

Camboglanna (present-day Castlesteads) was a Roman fort on Hadrian's
Wall. The neighbouring forts were Banna (Birdoswald) to the east and
Uxelodunum (Stanwix) to the west. In 1934, the site was partially excavated,
and the walls (apart from the missing north-east wall) were uncovered. The
north-east and south-west double gates, and the tower at the southern
corner, were also unearthed. It was suggested that a single ditch defended
the fort. Archaeologists have found and preserved several altars at the site.

The Eurasian bullfinch is a common winter bird. The male bullfinches
can be easily recognized by their flaming red underparts.

Septentrio

The door hinges creak
as the Goths scale the high walls
on a moonless night

Commentary

In ancient Roman religion, Septentrio was the name for the wind which comes directly from the north. The setting of the haiku poem above is the 5th century, and it depicts the siege of an Italian city by the Ostrogoths. The strong northern wind blows as the barbarians (also invading from the north) scale the city walls.

Pudicitia

A well-dressed maiden
greeted by gallant *vigils*;
the streets turn snow-white

Impudicitia

A half-dressed maiden
followed by his lustful eyes;
the cherry-red sky

Commentary

In ancient Rome, *pudicitia* was the virtue of modesty and proper sexual conduct. Its opposite was *impudicitia*, sexual shamelessness.

In religious terms, Pudicitia is also the divine personification of women's chastity and modesty. Her cult was exclusive of all but women who had married only once, since ancient Romans idealized idealized women who were *univira*, meaning "one-man" woman, who belonged to only one husband during their lifetime. Livy reports that there were two temples of Pudicitia in Rome, the Temple of Pudicitia Patricia and the Temple of Pudicitia Plebeia. The former and original one was for women of the patrician class only. However, when Verginia, the daughter of Aulus Verginius (a Roman patrician), was removed from the temple because she married a plebeian consul, she and a group of plebeian matrons founded a shrine of Pudicitia for women of the plebeian class as well. Livy mourned the decline in moral standards of followers of the cult by his time.

Pietas

A young patrician
bows low to the senator
as the session starts

Commentary

In ancient Rome, *pietas* was one of the principal virtues. Someone who has *pietas* exhibits the qualities of devotion, loyalty, and filial piety.

In religious terms, Pietas was a divine personification of a respectful and faithful attachment to gods, country, superiors, and relatives, especially parents. Pietas had a temple in Rome, consecrated in 181 BCE, and was frequently depicted on coins as a female figure carrying a palm twig and a sceptre, or as a matron casting incense upon an altar, sometimes accompanied by a stork, which was the symbol of filial piety.

The haiku poem above illustrates the practical application of *pietas* – a young politician offers his respectful obeisances to an older and more experienced senator.

Gravitas

The Caesar's stern look
as the unruly mob moans;
they all fall silent

Commentary

In ancient Rome, *gravitas* was one of the principal virtues. Someone who has *gravitas* exhibits the qualities of seriousness, dignity, self-control, and a sense of responsibility. Such a person does not easily give in to frivolous behaviour or excessive levity.

The haiku poem above illustrates the practical application of this virtue. For ancient Romans, *gravitas* was one of the main prerequisites for being a good leader. Regardless of whether one was a military tribune or a consul, an attitude of solemn dignity was highly praised.

Firmitas

Their benumbed, cold feet
as they march determinedly
through the plains of Gaul

Commentary

In ancient Rome, *firmitas* was one of the principal virtues. Someone who has *firmitas* exhibits the qualities of tenacity, firmness, and perseverance. The haiku poem above illustrates the practical application of this virtue. Despite hunger, cold, and fatigue, Julius Caesar's legionaries determinedly march through Gaul. During his campaign in Gaul, Caesar was known for his extremely rapid advances done to manoeuvre around enemy formations. Had it not been for the virtue of *firmitas* exemplified by his soldiers, the conquest and subjugation of Gaul would not have been possible.

Frugalitas

The old emperor
eats rye from a wooden bowl;
the soldiers' awed look

Commentary

In ancient Rome, *frugalitas* was one of the principal virtues. Someone who has *frugalitas* exhibits the qualities of frugality, simplicity, sobriety, and temperance. The Stoic philosopher and emperor Marcus Aurelius spoke highly of simplicity in his famous work *Meditations*.

The haiku poem above illustrates the practical application of this virtue. The old emperor is Marcus Aurelius himself, who shares the dining table with his soldiers. Rather than indulging in unnecessary luxury and delicacies, the emperor prefers a frugal ration of rye porridge.

Clementia

The crowd holds its breath
as the emperor rises;
the thumbs-up gesture

Commentary

In ancient Rome, *clementia* was one of the principal virtues. Someone who has *clementia* exhibits the qualities of benevolence, mercifulness, gentleness, and forbearance. The haiku poem above illustrates the practical application of this virtue. During ancient gladiatorial games, it was a customary practice for spectators to pass judgment on a defeated gladiator by giving the sign of a turned thumb (*pollice verso*). However, scant historical sources make it impossible to conclude whether the thumb was turned up, turned down, held horizontally, or concealed inside the hand to indicate a positive or negative judgement. In the poem above, the Roman emperor grants mercy to the fallen gladiator by using the thumbs-up sign.

Ataraxia

Mark Antony's speech
arouses the mourning crowd;
the sage stays quiet

Commentary

The haiku poem above illustrates the Stoic virtue of *ataraxia*, which is a state of inner tranquillity and freedom from disturbance by external events. The poem was inspired by William Shakespeare's tragedy *Julius Caesar*. In the play, after the assassination of Julius Caesar, Mark Antony is allowed to make a funeral oration (beginning with the famous phrase "Friends, Romans, countrymen, lend me your ears"). He uses rhetoric skills to depict Caesar in such a positive light that the mob becomes infuriated with the conspirators. Popular demagogues and politicians have always unethically exploited human psychology. Therefore, a man of the Stoic constitution should think twice before he gives in to any strong emotions experienced by crowds.

Sympatheia

The falling roof slate
kills the slave and his master;
ash buries them all

Commentary

The haiku poem above illustrates the Stoic concept of *sympatheia*, which refers to the interconnectivity and mutual interdependence of all things in the universe. The Stoic philosophers, particularly Marcus Aurelius, emphasized the affinity of parts to the organic whole on both social and cosmic levels. Contrary to what some utopian thinkers believe, it is impossible to attain absolute unity and equality of mankind, for there are evident biological, cultural, linguistic, or class differences between people. In the end, however, death makes everyone equal – both the slave and his master die during the eruption of Mount Vesuvius. Therefore, it is essential not to forget that we are all connected and share the same substance (*atman* or the higher Self, soul).

KAROL KOLBUSZ

De Brevitate Vitae

Rosy-cheeked children
blithely playing in the snow;
an ear-splitting scream

Commentary

The title of the haiku poem above (meaning "On the Shortness of Life") refers to a moral essay written by Seneca the Younger, who was a Roman Stoic philosopher.

Non omnis moriar

Derelict graveyard —
a stone seraph points his hand
at the leaden sky

Commentary

The Latin phrase *non omnis moriar* means "I shall not wholly die" and was coined by the Roman poet Horace. In his *Odes*, Horace refers to the permanence of an artist's work, which ensures immortality in the memory of posterity. A poet does not die completely – though his body is mortal, his art remains long after his passing. Horace believes that the poetry he created will survive generations, that it will prove to be more long-lasting than if he erected a bronze monument. The poets of subsequent generations referred to the theme of immortality through art, as it enabled them to draw inspiration for their creative work.

PART FOUR

DHARMIC HERITAGE

(VEDIC, BUDDHIST, JAIN, BÖN, AND SHINTŌ TRADITIONS)

Himalayan Temple

Little snowflake falls
from Ganesha's sunlit trunk
onto a small mouse

Commentary

In Sanatana Dharma, Ganesha (otherwise known as Ganapati) is the elephant-headed deity, the first son of Lord Shiva and Parvati. Ganesha is known as "remover of obstacles" (*vignaharta* in Sanskrit) and the god of auspicious beginnings; thus Sanatana Dharmis frequently invoke his name at the very start of rituals, ceremonies, or yoga practices. He is also considered to be the patron of learning and intellect. In iconographic depictions, Ganesha is often shown riding on or attended by a mouse, shrew or rat. Many different theories exist, all attempting to explain why this deity has a rodent as his vehicle (*vahana* in Sanskrit). According to one folk belief, it refers to his conquest of a pest that destroyed crops. Others interpret the mouse (with its ability to penetrate even the most hidden places) as a symbol of all-pervasiveness of Ganesha. The main religious festival dedicated to Ganesha is known as Ganesha Chaturthi. Observed in either August or September, it celebrates the arrival of the elephant-headed god from Shiva and Parvati's divine abode on Mount Kailash to our earthly realm.

Brahman

Abandoned temple —
stream of light pouring onto
Krishna's reddish lips

Commentary

In Vedic philosophy, Brahman is the metaphysical concept of the Absolute. It is the highest Universal Principle, which can be characterized as eternal, infinite, formless, transcendent, and not subject to change. Brahman is said to be the source of all auspiciousness, goodness, and supreme bliss. Brahman does not refer to the anthropomorphic concept of God known from the Abrahamic religions. However, according to the Vishishtadvaita ("qualified non-dualism") school of Vedic philosophy, Brahman is conceived as *Saguna Brahman* ("with qualities"), who possesses an infinite number of transcendental attributes. At the same time, he is also denominated *Nirguna Brahman* ("without qualities"), meaning that he is flawless (*nirdosatva*) and entirely devoid of qualities conditioned by matter. The haiku poem above refers to the all-pervasive (*sarva-gatam* in Sanskrit) quality of Brahman.

In the Vedic religion, Krishna is the eighth avatar (material incarnation) of the god Vishnu. Idols of Krishna (*murti*) usually depict him wearing a peacock-feather wreath and playing the flute, with his cherry-red lips drawn up in a mirthful smile. The worship of Krishna is most prominent in the Vaishnava tradition, though other denominations of Sanatana Dharma also hold him in sacred reverence. *The Bhagavad Gita*, one of the essential Vedic scriptures, recounts Krishna's appearance on earth and his philosophical dialogue with Prince Arjuna.

A Gift from God

At the window pane;
vapour from jasmine green tea
veils pale winter sun

Commentary

The word jasmine is of Persian origin and it means "god's gift". The white colour of jasmine symbolizes purity and spiritual illumination. It is also the national flower of Pakistan. Many temples in South Asia use jasmine in abundance.

Narasimha

A mountain lion jumps on the stocky brigand tearing him apart

Commentary

In the Vedic religion, Narasimha is the fourth avatar (material incarnation) of the god Vishnu. He is the half-lion, half-man fierce protector of *dharma* and destroyer of evil demons. Vishnu incarnated into the form of Narasimha in order to slay the demon Hiranyakashipu. The latter had obtained special powers which meant he could not be defeated during the day or night, inside or outside, by any weapon, nor by man or animal. Narasimha approached his foe at dusk (at the brink of day and night) at the threshold of a courtyard (neither indoors nor outdoors), and placed the demon on his thighs (neither on the ground nor in the air). Using his sharp nails (neither animate nor inanimate) as weapons, he ripped open the belly of the demon.

According to some scholars, Vishnu hymn 1.154 of the *Rigveda* is one of the earliest references to Narasimha:

Vishnu affirms on high by his mightiness and he is like a terrible lion that ranges in the difficult places, yea, his lair is on the mountain-tops, he in whose three wide movements all the worlds find their dwelling-place.

Three Deaths: Tamas

The fine white powder
spilled on the narrow walkway;
crowd ignores the corpse

Commentary

In the ancient Vedic tradition, we encounter the very interesting concept of the three *gunas* – psychological modes characteristic to the matter (*prakriti*): *sattva, rajas,* and *tamas.* These qualities are inherently present in everything and everyone but in varying proportions. *Tamas* is the mode of imbalance, chaos, darkness, apathy, inertia, and dullness. When businessmen or popular celebrities are not busy rushing after gold (*rajasic* activities), they sink even lower, to the mode of *tamas.* Bewildered by the superficial glamour of the sensual pleasures, they participate in mind-numbing consumption and intoxicate themselves, as if they were animals. The "fine white powder" in the poem is a reference to cocaine – taking drugs is one of the best examples of undesirable activities that place us in the mode of tamas.

Three Deaths: Rajas

The businessman's case
in the pool of blood and sleet;
the wailing sirens

Commentary

In the ancient Vedic tradition, we encounter the very interesting concept of the three *gunas* – psychological modes characteristic to the matter (*prakriti*): *sattva*, *rajas*, and *tamas*. These qualities are inherently present in everything and everyone but in varying proportions. *Rajas* is the mode of passion, activity, excitement, energy, motion, and change. A person who is predominantly *rajasic* (thus driven by greed and selfishness, living under the illusory spell of matter) can, for example, become obsessed with frenetic money-making because he or she wants to buy new cars and gadgets all the time.

The businessman's case in the poem is a perfect illustration of *rajasic* mania for ceaseless (and mostly meaningless – not for the sake of subsistence, but only for the promise of material sense gratification) pursuit of money, so characteristic of our modern times. Red, depicted here in the form of blood, is one of the primary *rajasic* colours. It is important to note that the Vedic scriptures do not frown upon the acquisition and possession of wealth. They do, however, warn us against the lure of money which frequently leads to greed and neglect of spiritual practice.

Three Deaths: Sattva

Quiet devotees —
warm sunlight on the pale neck
adorned with rose wreaths

Commentary

In the ancient Vedic tradition, we encounter the very interesting concept of the three *gunas* – psychological modes characteristic to the matter (*prakriti*): *sattva*, *rajas*, and *tamas*. These qualities are inherently present in everything and everyone but in varying proportions. *Sattva* is the mode of goodness, harmony, peace, tranquillity, purity, knowledge, and truth. One of many goals of spiritual practice is to cultivate the quality of *sattva*. When we eat healthy, fresh and nutritious food, when we exhibit positive character traits such as goodness, kindness, tolerance, wisdom, self-control, and calmness, when our thoughts are clear as the azure, midsummer sky, when our motives are pure as the perpetual snow on alpine peaks – then we are leading a *sattvic* lifestyle.

The haiku poem above describes the last moments of a saintly man or a guru (someone whose inner constitution is predominantly *sattvic*), who is surrounded by his faithful and well-wishing devotees. According to *The Bhagavad Gita*, one of the essential scriptures of Sanatana Dharma, the ultimate goal of spiritual practice, however, is to transcend all three qualities of material nature (*prakriti*) and realise our true, eternal *Self*, so that we can be "freed from birth, old age, disease, and death; and attain enlightenment". A person who has transcended the three *gunas* is known in Sanskrit as a *gunatita*.

Darukavana

Silent cedar trees
by the statue of Shiva;
slowly-falling snow

Commentary

Darukavana is the name of a sacred deodar forest mentioned in the *Shiva Purana*. Deodar, otherwise known as the Himalayan cedar, is revered as a holy tree consecrated to Lord Shiva. Shaivite sages used to reside and perform meditation in deodar forests, in order to please Lord Shiva (who is the personification of consciousness, as well as divine patron of Yoga and meditation). This tall tree, abundant in the western Himalayas, symbolizes the firmness and great strength of Shiva.

The poem refers to the temple to Shiva, located in the Tarkeshwar Mahadev village in India. Interestingly enough, right behind the temple, some deodar trees grow in the shape of *trishula* (trident), which is one of the most characteristic attributes of Shiva. On a subtler level of interpretation, the poem describes the qualities that emanate from a perfect yogi: silence (of the mind), firmness (discipline and unwavering attitude), tranquillity and purity (symbolized by slowly falling snow).

Ahimsa

The cross-legged Jain —
a fly lands on his red nose,
breath drives it away

Himsa

The scrawny horse plods
up the snow-covered mountain;
the crack of a whip

Commentary

Ahimsa (Sanskrit "non-violence", "non-harming") is one of the key virtues common to Sanatana Dharma, Buddhism, and Jainism. It is one of the five *yamas*, ethical principles of right living, mentioned by Patanjali in his *Yoga Sutras*.

Contrary to popular belief, *ahimsa* cannot be equated with pacifism, allowing victimhood, or displaying attitudes of passive submissiveness. Rather, cultivating this virtue means that we try to avoid inflicting violence (not only by deeds but also by words and in thoughts) on human beings and to minimise the amount of harm we cause to animals and the natural environment (as much as is practical). Furthermore, it is said that any form of violence tightens our karmic bondage, preventing us from freeing ourselves from the circle of rebirths. Motivated by this belief, many followers of Dharmic religions decide to abstain from eating meat.

The first poem illustrates, in a humorous way, the principle of *ahimsa* in practice. *Himsa* (Sanskrit "injury", "violence") is the opposite of *ahimsa*. The second poem depicts an agriculturalist (*vaishya*), perhaps driven by nothing but profit, who does not care about the well-being of his horse.

Lobha

The golden bracelet
glints in the apricity;
the thief's arched eyebrows

Commentary

Lobha is the Sanskrit word meaning "covetousness", "avarice". The haiku poem above depicts a scene happening in a marketplace at dusk. A thief, driven by greed for gold, spots the golden bracelet on someone's arm. Now he is wondering how to steal it without being seen. Such a misled person, detached from God and other human beings, is suffering from the illusion of scarcity. It is said that even oceans may be filled to the full with water, but *lobha* is an insatiable desire.

In the Vedic tradition, *lobha* is one of the six enemies of mind (*arishadvarga*), which prevent a person from attaining Self-realization. They bind the soul to the process of birth and death and keep it confined in this material world. Conversely, when we cultivate within us the direct opposites of *arishadvarga*, the bonds of our karmic captivity loosen.

Mada

The bodybuilder
looks in the ornate mirror
while his daughter cries

Commentary

Mada is the Sanskrit word meaning "pride", "conceit", or "stubborn-mindedness". The haiku poem above depicts a narcissistic bodybuilder who is obsessed with his temporal Self (*ahamkara*), and attached to his luxurious riches (the ornate mirror) to such an extent that he neglects the needs of his closest ones. Unfortunately, too many modern athletes fall into the trap of *mada*. According to the theory of masculine overcompensation, when men are insecure about their own gender identity, they will display overly masculine traits as compensation. The best remedy against an excess of arrogance and conceit is to dedicate our workouts to God and perceive one's body only as an auxiliary instrument of the higher, eternal Self (*atman*). It is essential to take proper care of our bodies by keeping them in good shape and health. However, we should never connect our true identity with something as imperfect and temporal as matter.

In the Vedic tradition, *mada* is one of the six enemies of mind (*arishadvarga*), which prevent a person from attaining Self-realization. They bind the soul to the karmic process of birth and death and keep it confined in this material world. Conversely, when we cultivate within us the direct opposites of *arishadvarga*, the bonds of our karmic captivity loosen.

Krodha

Abandoned palace —
scattered shards of pottery
on the snowy stairs

Commentary

Krodha is the Sanskrit word meaning "rage", "fury", or "indignation". Anger contaminates the senses and the intellect. According to *The Bhagavad Gita*, one of the essential scriptures of Sanatana Dharma, once our whole being is polluted, we become negligent in fulfilling our ethical and social obligations. In the history of mankind, many catastrophes could have been avoided, had it not been for the disastrous consequences of unchecked anger. The haiku poem above depicts a ruined palace, located high in the Himalayas, where a tragedy caused by someone's rage had likely happened.

In the Vedic tradition, *krodha* is one of the six enemies of mind (*arishadvarga*), which prevent a person from attaining Self-realization. They bind the soul to the karmic process of birth and death and keep it confined in this material world. Conversely, when we cultivate within us the direct opposites of *arishadvarga*, the bonds of our karmic captivity loosen.

Matsarya

The wild-eyed student
pours poison in the chalice;
the guru snoozes

Commentary

Matsarya is the Sanskrit word meaning "envy", "jealousy". The haiku poem above depicts a disciple who proceeds to poison his sleeping guru, out of envy and malice. He does not want to acknowledge his teacher's superiority and wisdom. In his youthful arrogance and spite taken to the extreme, the student is determined to get rid of the guru in order to take his place.

In the Vedic tradition, *matsarya* is one of the six enemies of mind (*arishadvarga*), which prevent a person from attaining Self-realization. They bind the soul to the karmic process of birth and death and keep it confined in this material world. Conversely, when we cultivate within us the direct opposites of *arishadvarga*, the bonds of our captivity loosen.

Moha

The bewildered man
gapes at the crystal palace
past Lakshmi's murti

Commentary

Moha is the Sanskrit word meaning "delusory emotional attachment" or "infatuation". The haiku poem above depicts a man who is bewildered by the deceptive power of possessing wealth and worldly prosperity, which are symbolized by the crystal palace. According to the Vedic scriptures, however, God is the ultimate owner and sustainer of all things on Earth. Those who deny this fact become beclouded with arrogance and greed, which leads them to their final downfall. Therefore, it is crucial to offer our thanks to Lakshmi, an ancient Indian goddess of abundance, wealth, and good fortune.

In the Vedic tradition, *moha* is one of the six enemies of mind (*arishadvarga*), which prevent a person from attaining Self-realization. They bind the soul to the karmic process of birth and death and keep it confined in this material world. Conversely, when we cultivate within us the direct opposites of *arishadvarga*, the bonds of our captivity loosen.

Kama

The toothless beggar
whistles at the slender queen
riding in the cart

Commentary

Kama is the Sanskrit word meaning "lust", "desire", or "pleasure of the senses". The haiku poem above depicts a pitiless vagrant who becomes lustful at the sight of a beautiful queen. *The Bhagavad Gita*, one of the essential scriptures of Sanatana Dharma, describes *kama* as "the sinful, all-devouring enemy in the world". Lust is not just uncontrolled sexual desire; it can also take the form of an obsessive craving for power, prestige, and money. Much like anger (which is the consequence of insatiate lust), these carnal desires becloud our reason and lead us to impulsive, foolish, and undesirable decisions.

In the Vedic tradition, *kama* is one of the six enemies of mind (*arishadvarga*), which prevent a person from attaining Self-realization. They bind the soul to the karmic process of birth and death and keep it confined in this material world. Conversely, when we cultivate within us the direct opposites of *arishadvarga*, the bonds of our captivity loosen.

Dharana

A little pine cone
falls onto a yogi's head;
his eyes remain closed

Commentary

Dharana is the Sanskrit word meaning "holding", "concentration", "firmness" or "steady focus". It is the sixth of the *Eight Limbs of Yoga* as described by Patanjali in the *Yoga Sutras*. *Dharana*, understood here as the art of attaining powerful concentration on a single point, is an ability that every sincere practitioner of Yoga must master in order to reap the full benefits of meditation. In the Vedic epic poem *Mahabharata*, this essential skill is demonstrated in an archery competition organised by guru Dronacharya, in which the noble prince Arjuna focused on the eye of the wooden bird. In contrast, his opponents concentrated on something other than the target itself.

The haiku poem above illustrates the principle of *dharana* – the yogi is so focused on his inner spiritual practice that nothing coming from the external world can disturb his perfect concentration.

Bhoot

His lonely vigil —
the scent of burned turmeric
lingers in the air

Commentary

In Vedic folklore, *bhoot* is the ghost of a deceased person. Much like in the Western tradition, *bhoots* are usually victims of violent death or suicide, which prevents them from moving on and not harassing the living. Oftentimes *bhoots* haunt specific houses (*bhoot bangla*), which are typically places where they died or which have some other significance to the ghost. They tend to inhabit *tamasic* spaces, such as abandoned buildings, ruins, or cemeteries. It is said that the scent of burned turmeric wards off these supernatural creatures. On a deeper level of interpretation, *bhoot* represents subtle psychological energies, inherent in both living and deceased persons.

Maha Shivaratri

Ash-marked devotees
meditate in pitch darkness
as the camphor burns

Commentary

Maha Shivaratri (Sanskrit: "the Great Night of Shiva") is the most favourable night of the year for worshipping Lord Shiva. This festival, famous for its introspective character, is celebrated annually in late winter (in either February or March). Devotees paint their faces with *tilaka* marks (traditionally prepared with sacred ash from *yajnas*, fire sacrifices) and observe an all-night meditative vigil while chanting hymns and mantras in praise of Lord Shiva. Some of them choose to fast during the day preceding the auspicious night. The fragrance and resin of camphor are frequently used in the worship of Shiva, who is said to be *Karpuragauram*, "pure like camphor".

Samatva

A pious Swami
looks at the king and a dog;
his calm, unmoved eyes

Commentary

Samatva is the Sanskrit concept meaning "equanimity". In *The Bhagavad Gita*, one of the essential scriptures of Sanatana Dharma, Lord Krishna describes *samatva* as even-mindedness to pleasure and pain, gain and loss, success and failure, as well as honour and disgrace. Furthermore, a sincere practitioner of yoga perceives both political leaders and beggars, elders and children, or elephants and dogs with an equal, compassionate eye. The principle of *samatva* cannot be equated with indifference or the lack of discernment, but rather understanding that each living being possesses the same eternal Self, *atman*.

The figure of *Swami* (Sanskrit word for "religious teacher") in the poem was inspired by Srila Prabhupada, one of the greatest Vaishnava gurus of the 20th century, who had significantly contributed to the spread of Sanatana Dharma in the Western world.

Madhu Vidya

Sweetness of honey
on the disciple's closed lips;
the guru's whisper

Commentary

Madhu Vidya (Sanskrit "honey-knowledge) is an essential esoteric concept in the Upanishadic scriptures of Sanatana Dharma. *Madhu Vidya* is a secret doctrine, communicated orally by the guru to the disciple, the knowledge and comprehension of which leads to supreme bliss. It is also related to the spiritual principle of *Soma*, the metaphorical nectar of peace, contentment, and immortality. According to the *Brihadaranyaka Upanishad*:

"The Self is the honey of all things, and all beings are the honey of the self. The radiant, immortal person who is in the self, or – in respect of oneself – the radiant, immortal person who is the self, is the self. This is the immortal, Brahman, the all."

Dhanvantari's Blessing

The doctor's prayer —
flushes of heat disappear
as the new dawn breaks

Commentary

Dhanvantari is a Vedic god, an incarnation of Vishnu, closely associated with Ayurveda (Vedic medicine) and the healing of body, mind, and spirit. Many hospitals and clinics in India regard him as their patron deity. According to legend, when the Devas and Asuras were churning the oceans of the world, he emerged out of the depths carrying a vessel filled with *amrita*, the elixir of immortality that could cure all diseases. Subsequently, Dhanvantari began to teach the art and science of Vedic medicine. *The Puranas* acknowledge him as the god of Ayurveda. The haiku poem above depicts an Ayurvedic physician who is praying to Dhanvantari for his patient's quick recovery.

Madyaakshepa

The bewildered king
leans out of the top window;
wine mixed with red snow

Commentary

Charaka Samhita, an ancient Ayurvedic manual, mentions that alcohol abuse (*madyaakshepa*) can affect the intellectual functions of grasping new concepts, retaining information, and memory. A major reason for drinking alcohol is to change our mood and mental state. Therefore, people with various psychological and emotional problems (including mere stress) seek refuge in this substance. However, the relief is only temporary. Every sincere seeker of Truth should not only keep away from drunkenness but also consider quitting alcohol altogether. There is absolutely no reason to alter our consciousness with toxic substances in the hope of getting a fleeting feeling of false joy in return.

The haiku poem above depicts a drunk king who kills himself in an accident. The tremendous responsibility inherent to positions of leadership requires absolute control over one's speech and actions. Alcohol beclouds the reason, thus diminishing one's discernment and ability to make the right decisions.

Mount Kailash

The silent stupas —
a pilgrim looks at the peak
soaked in afterglow

Commentary

Mount Kailash is a prominent mountain located near the Chinese border with India and Nepal. The peak has religious significance in all four major religions in this part of Asia: Sanatana Dharma, Buddhism, Jainism, and Bön. It is believed that Mount Kailash is the abode of Lord Shiva and his family (including Parvati, Ganesha, and Skanda). Every year, thousands of pilgrims who adhere to the aforementioned religions circumambulate the mountain on foot in the sacred ritual of *kora*, in order to imbibe the divine energy of the peak. Some of these walkers prostrate themselves repeatedly over the entire length of the trail. Stupas are mound-like structures used for the veneration of Buddhist saints and relics.

Manasarovar

A bird's white feather
floats on the crystalline lake;
the mirrored twilight

Commentary

Lake Manasarovar is a high-altitude lake near Mount Kailash. The sacred reverence for the lake is common to all four major religions in this part of Asia: Sanatana Dharma, Buddhism, Jainism, and Bön. According to Vedic scriptures, Manasarovar is the outward manifestation of Lord Brahma's mind. Pilgrims from all over the world take ceremonial baths in the waters of the lake, which are believed to cleanse their sins. For it is said in the *Skanda Purana*:

"There are no mountains like the Himalaya, for in them are Kailash and Manasarovar. As the dew is dried up by the morning sun, so are the sins of man blotted out at the sight of the Himalayas."

Mauna

A fierce row breaks out
in front of the great guru
who keeps his lips sealed

Commentary

Mauna is the Sanskrit word meaning "silence" or "taciturnity". From the profane point of view, it refers to the practice of refraining from speaking or speaking less. It is undoubtedly a good idea to speak only when we have something important to communicate, for it is through speech that we waste the greatest amount of life energy or *prana*. However, from the subtler point of view, *mauna* alludes to the state of inner quietude and tranquillity, which is one of the goals of meditation.

The silence of the guru in the poem should not be interpreted as indifference to the argument happening in front of him or mere unwillingness to unnecessarily lose *prana*. Rather, his attitude is a statement in itself – a non-verbal response to the row.

Yeti

A snow-blind hermit
strays off the narrowing path;
a menacing growl

Commentary

In Himalayan folklore, Yeti (otherwise known as the "Abominable Snowman") is a legendary being resembling a hairy, ape-like creature, who is said to live in the highest and most remote parts of the Himalayas. The haiku poem above depicts a cave-dwelling hermit (*naljorpa*) who gets caught in the snowstorm. He is unable to find his way and eventually encounters a Yeti.

Tummo Yoga

He sits motionless
as stiff wind bites his pale cheeks;
fluffy snowflakes melt

Commentary

In Tibetan Buddhism, *Tummo Yoga* is an ancient meditation technique which consists of breathing and visualisation exercises, whose ultimate goal is to increase a person's "inner heat". This inner fire is believed to burn away the practitioner's ignorance and clinging to illusion (*maya*). According to Alexandra David-Néel's account in her book *Magic and Mystery in Tibet*, the cave-dwelling hermits (*naljorpas*) who live at the highest altitudes of the Himalayas have mastered *Tummo Yoga*. They are capable of increasing their body temperature, which is useful for keeping the body warm in cold weather conditions. Some methods used in *Tummo Yoga* are part of Wim Hof's famous breathing exercises.

The haiku poem above depicts the cave-dwelling hermit (*naljorpa*) from the previous poem. He has apparently evaded the peril of being torn apart by the Yeti. However, the blizzard still rages on. The monk stops and proceeds to meditate, harnessing the powerful psycho-physical energies of his body, which in the end save him from hypothermia.

As Above, So Below

A galloping horse
passes by white prayer flags;
the sick child gets well

Commentary

In Tibetan tradition, prayer flags are colourful cloth banners inscribed with prayers for peace and good fortune. They are traditionally strung either horizontally or vertically along halyards in high places and on mountain peaks so that the wind passing over the surface of the flags will carry away the auspicious blessings. The origins of this custom can be traced to the Bön religion. The wind horse (Tibetan *rlung rta*) is one of the most common symbols appearing on the prayer flags. It relates to luck and well-being.

The title of the poem refers to the traditional law of analogy, which emphasizes the correspondence between heaven and the earthly plane. In other words, what happens on one level of reality can also influence every other level. This sacred connection has been forgotten in the modern world, which labels such viewpoints as "superstitious". It was first formulated by Hermes Trismegistus in the *Emerald Tablet*.

"That which is Below corresponds to that which is Above, and that which is Above, corresponds to that which is Below, to accomplish the miracles of the One Thing."

Tangaryō

The cross-legged novice
at the monastery gate;
snow covers his feet

Commentary

In Zen Buddhism, *tangaryō* is a period of time spent sitting at the gate of a Zen monastery in anticipation of being accepted inside. It can last from one day to several weeks, depending on the quality of one's sitting.

Sesshin

The fast-moving clouds reflected in the windows; the monks are unstirred

Commentary

In Zen Buddhism, *sesshin* is a week-long period in the life of a monastery, when the daily schedule is almost exclusively restricted to intensive *zazen* (seated meditation) sessions. During *sesshin*, silence is observed, sleep is restricted to an absolute minimum (usually no longer than five hours), and meditation is only interrupted by short periods of communal work and meals.

The fast-moving clouds in the poem refer to the Buddhist doctrine of *anitya*, which refers to the impermanent and transitory nature of all things. Human beings, caught in the continuous flow of life, death, and rebirth (*samsāra*), experience dissatisfaction with themselves and their lives, inner restlessness, and suffering of conditioned existence (*sankhara-dukkha*). According to Buddhist teachings, the realization that there is no permanent, fixed Self (*anātman*) can contribute to one's liberation and enlightenment (*nirvana*). This viewpoint, however, stands in opposition to what is taught in different schools of Sanatana Dharma, as well as the earliest forms of Buddhism. They all recognize the existence of an eternal, permanent, and changeless Self (*atman*).

Kinhin

Their numb, silent feet
pace the wooden floor slowly
dappled in sunlight

Commentary

In Zen Buddhism, *kinhin* is a technique of rhythmic walking meditation synchronised with one's breath. Monks are recommended to do it between long periods of *zazen*, seated meditation. The walking meditation begins with forming the *mudra* (hand position) of *shashu*: the right hand is wrapped lightly about its thumb, the left hand covers the right, and they rest at the solar plexus. Then the practitioners slowly circumambulate the meditation hall for about 5 or 10 minutes. While relaxing one's muscles and stretching the legs might be important to one's health, it is only the secondary goal of *kinhin*. The primary focus is on integrating mindful awareness into more mundane activities of one's daily life. In this sense, *kinhin* can be perceived as a direct continuation of sitting meditation.

Karuna

The thin ice shatters
under the yelping puppy;
the monk springs forward

Commentary

In Theravāda Buddhism, *karuna* ("compassion") is one of the four *brahmavihārās* ("abodes of Brahma"), which are virtues and ethical principles. *Karuna* can be equated with being compassionate towards living beings, the universe, and oneself, as well as taking action to diminish the amount of suffering in the world. The haiku poem above demonstrates the virtue of *karuna* in practice, as compassion towards suffering animals is one of its key elements.

Upekkhā

The barking mongrels
surround the wandering monk;
dispassionate glance

Commentary

In Theravāda Buddhism, *upekkhā* ("equanimity") is one of the four *brahmavihārās* ("abodes of Brahma"), which are virtues and ethical principles. *Upekkhā* is the practice of disassociating one's consciousness from the undesirable fluctuations of the external world. It is not to be understood as indifference or apathy, but as a state of inner tranquillity and balance that cannot be easily disturbed by what happens on the outside. Equanimity allows us to walk evenly over the uneven, as the Buddha used to say.

The haiku poem above illustrates the principle of *upekkhā* in practice. The image of barking mongrels has been borrowed from the Stoic writings, for *upekkhā* is similar to the Stoic concept of *ataraxia*. Many scholars and researchers have highlighted numerous similarities between Buddhism and Stoicism.

Koan

Fluffy white snowflakes
gently fluttering upwards
towards the red clouds

Commentary

In Zen Buddhism, a *koan* is a brief, paradoxical anecdote, statement, or question given by a teacher to a disciple in the form of a riddle. They usually admit no logical solution. *Koans* are used to demonstrate the inadequacy of dualistic and logical patterns of thinking and to encourage monks to abandon their ultimate dependence on analytical reasoning. Buddhist monks are taught numerous *koans* so that they can eventually attain *satori*, which can be understood as acquiring a new point of view on the true nature of reality. Having awakened to *satori*, they become more receptive to enlightenment.

Zen Garden

The frozen frog pond —
mossy pathways of gravel
covered in light snow

Commentary

The Japanese rock garden is a type of dry-landscape garden, whose design is inspired by the philosophy and principles of Zen Buddhism. A well-designed Zen garden is an evocative work of art that draws the visitor into a state of mindful reflection and promotes a feeling of serenity and peacefulness. They were originally created outside Buddhist temples in order to aid monks in their contemplation upon the teachings of Buddha. The poem contains a reference and tribute to the famous haiku by Matsuo Bashō, who was the greatest master of haiku poetry:

an ancient pond
a frog jumps in
the splash of water

Kamidana

The candle wax melts
as the amulets flutter;
gloam in the window

Commentary

In the Shintō religion of Japan, *kamidana* is a miniature shrine inside houses. These altars are used for worshipping and revering *kami*, which are interpreted as spirits and essences present in natural phenomena. The front of the shrine contains the *taima*, an inscribed board from the main Shintō shrine at Ise, which symbolizes the universal *kami*. On either side of the altar are protective paper amulets called *o-fuda*. Consecrated to tutelary deities, they are meant to bring good fortune to those who place them in their household shrines. Oblations of food, *sake* (an alcoholic beverage made from fermented rice), water, and green twigs are placed daily at the centre of the shrine.

Tsuri-dōrō

The hanging lanterns
swing in the blustery dusk;
a forgotten shrine

Commentary

In traditional Japanese architecture, *tsuri-dōrō* (otherwise known as *kaitomoshi*) is a type of a hanging lantern made of stone, wood, or metal. These lanterns are usually suspended in rows from the eaves of a temple roof. In the Shintō religion, they were traditionally thought to prevent ancestor spirits from getting lost in the dark. The setting of the poem has been inspired by the Tōnomine Shrine, located in Nara Prefecture, Japan.

Itsukushima Shrine

The snow-capped torii
softly illuminated
by the sinking sun

Commentary

Itsukushima is a small island located in Hiroshima Bay, on Japan's west coast. It is the location of a famous Shintō shrine, best known for its monumental gate (*torii*) built over water, which appears to float during high tide. Interestingly enough, the main pillars of the gate are not set in the seabed but stand firmly due to their weight.

Anshin

A gnarled apple tree
casts its shadow on the wall
inside the old shrine

Commentary

In Japanese *anshin* is a word meaning "peace of mind" or "relief".

PART FIVE

MISCELLANEOUS POEMS

Cottage in Winter

The child is asleep —
a reflection of starlight
in the half-full glass

The Somnambulist

A glance of moonlight
in her blank, unseeing eyes
as she walks cliff-wards

Imprisoned Reflections

Moonlight in the well —
a meteorite falls in
and breaks through the ice

The Triad

Three cloaked silhouettes —
dark trees veiled in freezing fog
swirling above snow

The Visit

The star-studded sky —
a soft crunching of footsteps
on the snow outside

The Haunted Cathedral

The moonlight's cold lance
coming through the rose window;
sounds of hushed whispers

Serenity

Breeze on the calm lake —
swans in the aureate glow
of the setting sun

Carpathian Winter

A long-haired sheepdog
sleeps in the glare of the flames;
howling on the peaks

The Vampyre

The turn of the key —
a stream of silver moonlight
in the dusky vault

Melk

Dusk at the old farm —
sunlight brightens the dark smoke
from the brick chimney

Progress

Grinding of the gears
blocks out the sound of crying;
the dull, smoggy sky

Lullaby

A vagrant's tired face
in the gleam of moonlit snow;
an old, damp cellar

Abandoned Attic

Distant church bells chime —
snow comes through the rose window
while the candle glows

Winter Idyll

Silent afternoon —
a tabby cat in the fields
soaked in golden light

Imagination

Dim, silver moonlight
on the three marble gargoyles
in the old churchyard

Nocturne

The barking of dogs —
a burglar unsheathes his sword
as the moon comes out

The Final Solution

A chair goes missing
amid the sudden bedlam;
a nurse finds loose wire

The Exiles

Noctambulant shapes
loom out of the windswept moors;
the drumming of hooves

Cursed in Eternity

The abandoned keep
perches on the blackened rock;
a grey wraith appears

A Blaze in the Northern Sky

Waft of burning wood
in the frosty midnight air;
an arctic campfire

Funeral Fog

Two thugs raise their swords
as he enters the graveyard —
the fog veils their hands

Mistake

The breath of horses
shivering in the blizzard —
gaping stable gates

Foss

A pitch-black figure
leads the tall Swedish hermit
to the waterfall

The White Cloak

The naked birches —
wind gusts cover the bark with
freshly fallen snow

The Silent Hours

The narrow alley
filled with uncanny shadows;
grey cats in the sleet

First Love

Slight blush on her face
as she receives the letter;
tears stain the harsh words

Loneliness

The steamy window
obscures a saturnine face;
clamour on the streets

Understanding

Two silent figures
sitting by the fireplace;
their hands slowly meet

Sleeplessness

A white-gowned woman
gazes at the stormy sea
from her loft window

Disintegration

Two voiceless persons
sit at the dining table;
their faces are cold

The Drowning Man

The airhole bubbles —
the babbling men turn their sight
from the sinking arms

Absence

The peasant's kitchen —
a bowl of cold potatoes
in the evening gloom

Ice-Crowned

Waiting for her date —
pendent icicles shatter
and fall on her head

Friday Afternoon

The clock is ticking —
light recedes from the kitchen
as the sun goes down

Haste

A sip of coffee
spilled on the oaken table;
its smell still lingers

Dangers of Laziness

A cat on the porch
purring in sweet drowsiness;
a mouse slips away

Closedown

Last rays of the sun
on the forest canopy;
the birds are silent

The Parting

In his cold embrace —
she stares at the distant peaks
clad in snow and ice

Dawn at the Farm

A trail of fresh blood
left on the powdery snow;
shreds of rabbit fur

Prey

A weary red fox
on the desolate meadows —
an eagle swoops down

Abandoned House

Forsaken cobwebs
hidden behind lace curtains;
a skull on the ledge

Sorrow

The sound of cellos
in a dimly lit chamber —
the falling snowflakes

Emptiness

A forsaken swing
in the snow-covered orchard;
the cold air is still

No Trespassing

A pack of stray dogs
roaming across the dark fields;
the noise of gunshots

Station to Station

A quiet noontide —
the roar of a passing train
startles the roe deer

Winter Ghosts

Old, abandoned barn —
a sunlit, rusty padlock
creaks in the cold wind

False Dawn

The anxious mother
looks fixedly at the light
on the horizon

The Passing

An old hare sits still
in the hoary fields of frost;
wind ruffles its fur

Decrepitude

A gloomy forenoon —
wind moans through lonely fences
rotting on the hills

The Last Day of Winter

Patches of blueness
appear in the sombre sky;
the snow is melting

FURTHER READING

The following section contains a list of works which the reader may consult for additional information and context about the religious or historical traditions depicted in the poems.

Celtic heritage

L. Alcock – *Arthur's Britain*
M. Aldhouse-Green – *Dictionary of Celtic Myth and Legend*
N. Chadwick – *The Celtic Realms*
B. Cunliffe – *The Ancient Celts*
B. Cunliffe – *Iron Age Communities in Britain*
P. Ellis – *The Druids*
M. Green – *Animals in Celtic Life and Myth*
I. A. Gregory – *Gods and Fighting Men*
I. A. Gregory – *Visions and Beliefs in the West of Ireland*
P. Monaghan – *The Encyclopedia of Celtic Myth and Folklore*
J. Koch – *Celtic Culture. A Historical Encyclopedia*
T. F. O'Rahilly – *Early Irish History and Mythology*

Germanic heritage

Beowulf
H. R. Ellis Davidson – *Gods and Myths of Northern Europe*
H. R. Ellis Davidson – *The Lost Beliefs of Northern Europe*
H. R. Ellis Davidson – *The Road to Hell*
G. Dumézil – *Gods of the Ancient Northmen*
J. Grimm – *Teutonic Mythology*
C. Tacitus – Germania

Greek and Roman heritage

M. Beard – *Religions of Rome*
W. Burkert – *Greek Religion*
G. Dumézil – *Archaic Roman Religion*
Epictetus – *Discourses*
E. Gibbon – *The Decline and Fall of Roman Empire*
Homer – *The Iliad*
Homer – *The Odyssey*
Marcus Aurelius – *Meditations*

Polybius – *Histories*
G. Suetonius – *On Famous Men*
G. Suetonius – *The Twelve Caesars*
R. Turcan – *Gods of Ancient Rome*
Xenophon – *Anabasis*

Dharmic Heritage

D. P. Acharya – *Sanatana Dharma: The Eternal Natural Way*
A. David-Néel – *Magic and Mystery in Tibet*
D. Frawley – *Shiva: The Lord of Yoga*
Krishna – *The Bhagavad Gita*
D. T. Suzuki – *An Introduction to Zen Buddhism*
D. T. Suzuki – *The Training of the Zen Buddhist Monk*
The Upanishads
M. Yamakage – *The Essence of Shinto*